ABOUT THE AUTHOR

Julia McCoy is an 8x author and a leading strategist around creating exceptional content and presence that lasts online. As the VP of Marketing at Content at Scale, she leads marketing for one of the fastest-growing AI content writing tools for SEO marketers on the planet. She's been named in the top 30 of all content marketers worldwide, is the founder of Content Hacker, and exited a 100-person writing agency she spent 10 years building with a desire to help marketers, teams, and entrepreneurs find the keys of online success and revenue growth without breaking.

Read her eight books on Amazon, including a non-fiction memoir of her life growing up in and escaping a radical cult: Woman Rising, A True Story.

Connect with Julia on Twitter and Instagram: @JuliaEMcCoy.

Visit Julia's site: ContentHacker.com

Learn about Content at Scale: ContentHacker.com/AI or ContentatScale.ai

Email the author: julia@contenthacker.com

Dedicated to my online readers. Without you, I wouldn't have a reason to keep writing.

TABLE OF CONTENTS

INTRODUCTION 1

CHAPTER 1: How to Get into a High-Performing
Content Writing Headspace 7

CHAPTER 2: Email Writing + Special AI Feature: ... 37
    AI Writing with ChatGPT for Email Copy

CHAPTER 3: Social Media Writing + Special AI
Feature: 89
    Twitter Threads with ChatGPT

CHAPTER 4: SEO Blog Writing + Special AI Feature: 113
    AI + Content Tutorial to 5-10x Your Blog
    Writing Speed

CHAPTER 5: Sales Page Writing + Special AI Feature: 181
    Using Jasper and Content at Scale for Sales Copy

CHAPTER 6: Writing for YouTube + Special AI
Feature: 223
    ChatGPT Prompts for YouTube Outliness

CONCLUSION 245

ABOUT THE AUTHOR 247

INTRODUCTION

PICTURE IT.

I could hear the oh-so-obvious pain in her voice.

I was talking to a tenured entrepreneur on Zoom. Knowledge was oozing out of her. She and her husband had both served their growing clientele from a beautiful office in Arizona for nearly two decades. Together, they managed a financial group and consulted clients.

"We had 500 people open the email out of 3,000."

There was a long pause.

"No one signed up and registered. Out of those 500 that opened the email—no one signed up."

Another long, sad pause. I held that moment with her, sitting there and frowning. I felt her pain, so deeply—but I also knew the remedy, and I was biting my tongue. I knew she was about to tell me the remedy herself. For goodness' sake, she valued good content and knew its worth—she'd followed me and my work at Content Hacker for a couple of years now.

"It was the content."

Another pause. "Well—" she quickly adjusted, "That or the timeframe didn't work for anyone."

I've had people from Australia stay up until one a.m. for my events, so I knew better. I reinforced her first thought: "It was the content. Content quality makes or breaks you. We have to adapt from essay to internet." Then, I added: "I'm not saying we're going to 'millennialize' Tom or insult his expertise. We're going to *present* his expertise in a way that people will actually *read* it." Tom, her husband, was a bonafide investment expert who *hated* the "millennial" style of writing—as he called it. (I chuckled, hearing that. *I'm* a millennial. And I still hate the half-arsed style of writing that some content writers like to pass off as "new age" or "good." Nope. Sloppiness doesn't "upgrade" your content; it downgrades it. Great content is a unique formula of **care, expertise,** and **optimization.** You must have all three—and there is nothing sloppy in any one of those three.

"Yes. This is why I need you."

She was in my mentorship program at Content Hacker, attended all the monthly Zooms and had soaked in every bit of content marketing wisdom from our community. She'd been trying to get her team to write in the style online readers actually read, but it wasn't working. For goodness' sake, they were financial experts; not savvy 2020s-reader-friendly content writers. She'd been trying to increase conversions, but things on her website and email list were falling *dead flat.*

It took kahunas just for her to admit that no one signed up from their email blast.

Because that's simply *outrageous,* given their expertise—not to mention incredibly painful. No expert in her shoes should have to see content fall flat again, and again, and again, but it happens.

Why?

Most of the time—the answer is very simple.

The content was total crap. Whoever wrote it had *no* understanding of how to write for an online audience.

The solution is not so simple. You must train your writer (whether using AI or not—preferably, *with* AI) or train yourself how to write *better* content. The *best* content equals the *best* results.

Fast-forward from my summer of 2022 conversation, over into a not-so-distant future full of change. January 2023.

Artificial intelligence had suddenly leaped to the forefront of my industry.

OpenAI (creator of GPT-3, 4, etc.) had launched ChatGPT, and it was all the hype. Over a million users had signed up for it in nine days. It gained so much notoriety, people you wouldn't expect to use it *did.* (My uncle used ChatGPT to write a poem on the spot about herding bison—get this, with cowboys at a campfire in the deep country. Hilarious.)

AI writing tools that were glorified API calls into OpenAI's GPT-3 (soon to be 4) were launching left and right. I tried a bunch, and of course, ChatGPT: but I hadn't been thrilled with it for long-form content. For short form: Awesome. A definite aide. A huge tool in your toolkit. (See our section in this book from Owen Hemsath, who is using ChatGPT to help generate awesome YouTube scripts and outlines for industry-leading clients of his.) My concern with ChatGPT for long-form and website content was the lack of factual accuracy. OpenAI itself has said ChatGPT is based on no source of truth; it's B.S.es you half the time. But, the *billions of data points* it has access to means *billions of unique ways to frame and say sentences.* With "nothing new under the sun," almost all content is a rewrite or reposition of an existing thought, anyways; it's just that OpenAI's technology can now say it in a billion different ways—and a human will never be capable of that. Never. That's a wild thought.

I knew that OpenAI and ChatGPT would forever change the game, but I didn't know *how much* it would—because I was still using MS Office Word to start my full-length blogs. I couldn't introduce a tool yet into the SEO writing process, because it was impossible. ChatGPT's data and facts for blogging were way off. It didn't pull current data from the top of Google. It didn't know how to deep-research and find statistics and information that content writers vitally need to find and rely on for high-quality, comprehensive informative articles. The specific list of "what's missing" went on, and on. I explored it at length, pitting my own human writer against ChatGPT and finding the content it writes seriously lacking in quality and accuracy.

All of that changed when I found a tool called **Content at Scale.** It *actually wrote* the kind of content that rivaled my best writer—with accuracy, quality, and depth. (With some quirks and target misses here and there—but that's any software. Just re-run it.) I found Content at Scale while watching a YouTube video by Adam Enfroy, a top affiliate blogger. We'll talk about the use of Content at Scale as a long-form AI writing tool more inside the pages of this book, but for now, suffice it to say that after a single call with its visionary founder Justin McGill, I took an amazing role he offered me as VP of Marketing and the rest is history. I'm now in the mix of *thousands* of use cases and incredible opportunities to help marketers, freelancers, teams, and business owners navigate the use of AI writing while staying relevant and human with their audiences.

It's a dream. Has it been easy? No. I've had to learn, from scratch, what it means to be part of a team where I'm *not* the sole founder and owner. That transition alone has been charged with all kinds of emotional weight, but the beauty coming from it: the *home* that all my unique, nerdy, well-honed skills have found inside this company.

Do I still believe in the exact sentence I wrote prior to this lightning-fast change of adapting to AI in January of 2023? → **You must train your writer, or train yourself, on how to write *better* content. The *best* content equals the *best* results.**

Yes, yes, I do.

1,000 blogs… 10 years of writing… 8 books, plus one every year… 40,000 content projects for clients… the rapid recognition and growth of the companies I've either run, consulted, or worked at (Express Writers, Content Hacker, Content at Scale) …

I've always staked my name on writing the **best** content.

And I will continue to.

That's why this book remains an in-depth, human guide on *how to write*; built so that you understand content before you understand incredibly powerful tools like Content at Scale (which will write correct headers, optimize the content with the right keywords, and do all the heavy lifting *for* you in writing)—i.e., understand good content *before* you run the AI engine. This will help you be a far better **AIO** (artificial intelligence optimizer) writer, strategist, or creator; and adapt to the new world of AI writing with ease.

I've always believed that the fastest way to overcome imposter syndrome is by **learning the skill.** That's one big reason why this book remains skill-first in approach.

This is a simple, easy, highlight-worthy handbook that will train you to do one thing.

Write better content. (With AI in your process to dramatically speed up time.)

Enjoy.

CHAPTER 1:

How To Get Into A High-Performing Content Writing Headspace

If you're familiar with any of my teachings, training, or courses, you know I always start with mindset. And this is where we will start once again, long before we get deep into the nitty-gritty steps of writing incredible content that performs like Babe Ruth at his career height.

To put it in blunt terms, **mindset affects everything**. If you're a writer, that includes your profession—your writing. And if you're stuck in a mindset that says, "I'm not good enough," "I'm not as skilled as XYZ writer," or "I'm never going to be [insert descriptor you want but don't feel worthy of]"…

Friend, we have some work to do.

We need to comb through your thought patterns and find out what's holding you back. And then we need to pack those Negative Ninas off on a one-way plane ride to the Arctic Circle.

Because **to write like a high-performing writer, you need to think like one**. And high-performing writers are *confident* about their skills. They regularly think, "I'm ENOUGH, and I've got this copy handled. Watch me fly."

See the difference?

They've got the mindset… and the skill set. The quickest way to beat imposter syndrome is to actually have the skill. And that's why before we talk about AI writing *at all*, we're going to cover the skill itself in-depth, so you understand this at a human (non-robot) level.

If you feel confident about your headspace, good going! This preface will still have some golden nuggets of truth to offer you, and maybe some reinforcement for what you already know in your gut.

If you're a business owner looking to train your writers on winning content, this part of the book is doubly important. Even though you're not a writer by profession, you've probably dabbled, and distilling these concepts will trickle down to your team.

And, if you nodded your head at every word of the previous paragraphs, I have some wisdom to lay on you from over 10 years in the trenches of content writing.

Why Your Writing Mindset Matters

In a study[1] of how mindset affects student achievement, the **number one predictor of success** was

---

[1] Mona Mourshed, Marc Krawitz, and Emma Dorn. (2017). "How to improve student educational outcomes: New insights from data analytics." McKinsey.

NOT the home environment, not behavior, not student or teacher factors, but… (drumroll) **mindset**.

Students who had a growth mindset—the belief that you can succeed if you work hard enough, that you can learn and improve your skills, intelligence, and behavior—performed 9-17% better than their counterparts with a fixed mindset—the belief that you can't change your capabilities.

Carol Dweck, the Stanford psychologist whose research defines and demonstrates the difference between the two mindsets,[2] found that growth-mindset students are also better equipped to leap over setbacks to reach their goals than their equally talented, fixed-mindset peers.

In other words, put a group of people together who are equally talented at a skill, and the best performing among them probably *won't* have some sort of secret leg up. Instead, the highest achievement will belong to the person who most believes in their individual growth and improvement—and acts on it. The person always on the lookout for "better" WILL be better.

It sounds cheesy to say, "You can achieve your dreams if you just believe!"—but science somehow turns this glitter-and-rainbows statement into fact. Your beliefs and attitudes are not just pieces of your personality, but also important determiners of how you'll perform in life.

---

https://www.mckinsey.com/industries/education/our-insights/how-to-improve-student-educational-outcomes-new-insights-from-data-analytics

[2] Marina Krakovsky. (2017, Sept.). "Why Mindset Matters." Stanford Magazine. https://stanfordmag.org/contents/why-mindset-matters

It makes sense. Mindset shapes your motivation, which in turn shapes the type of effort you put into tasks. It makes sense that people who don't give up, who believe they can improve, DO improve and succeed; and people who give up easily, who think poorly of their performance and believe they can't change it, DON'T improve and fail.

How does this tie back into content writing?

If your mindset bleeds into everything you do, then **your mindset while writing** is an elemental factor in everything you produce, whether that's a tiny line of copy for a Facebook ad or a hefty, meaty, 5,000-word blog post.

Think: When you were confident about your skill at writing that piece of copy, that blog post, how much easier was that task? How much more smoothly did it go? How much better did the final piece read? How much better did it *perform*?

Your confidence in your writing skill will be apparent in every word you commit to the page. Self-assured, competent writers have a unique style and flair in their writing. You know their voice because they own it and believe in it. Their pieces get rankings, shares, clicks, engagement, and more because, at least in part, this self-assuredness results in skilled copy and content.

I can think of a few writers in the content marketing space who fit this mold: Seth Godin, who can pen a blog post consisting of only 20 lines that contain oceanic depths; Ann Handley, whose spunky personality and wit sparkle on the page; Henneke

Duistermaat, who so elegantly and simply explains writing concepts alongside her whimsical, hand-drawn illustrations; and Jon Morrow, who is a master of the blogging medium and infuses it with a flair for storytelling.

None of these writers have similar styles. They all have different audiences, different content focuses, and diverging goals. But they ALL share that confidence behind their writing that's ultimately a result of mindset.

If you want to cultivate a similar mindset for greatness, you need a few components: belief that you're a work-in-progress, and the desire to improve.

Repeat After Me: I'm a Writer-in-Progress

I firmly believe the writer you are today will *NOT* be the writer you are tomorrow.

Even if you're not a great writer at this moment, the potential for greatness is still inside you.

You just have to work for it.

And, no, you'll *never* reach a day where you'll say, "Okay, that's it. I have officially learned everything there is to know about writing. Now I can stop."

Not a chance. You're a writer-in-progress from the first day you pick up a crayon and write your name in proud, crooked capital letters, to the time when you're uber-successful and writing to an enthralled audience from a cushy chair in your writing den. It's a train ride into infinity, *and that's okay.*

As you try on your own unique "writer-in-progress" hat and see how it fits, remember there are habits that will reinforce your never-ending road to improvement. These are my favorite, and, I think, the most effective.

The writer's hat material

1. *Read Every Day*

Reading is the ultimate training tool for writers. Any scribe worth their feathered pen will read regularly and widely.

That's because good readers are good writers.

Reading is THE single activity that has the power to do all this:

It grows your vocabulary. Research shows[3] there is no better way to learn new words.

[3] Todd Brinson. (2019, May.). "Neuroscience explains the astonishing benefits of reading books like a writer—even if you don't plan on becoming one." CNBC.
https://www.cnbc.com/2019/03/27/neuroscience-explains--how-successful-people-read-books.html

It strengthens your ability to imagine and empathize with all kinds of people and situations. How else could you experience first-hand what it's like to grow up in the deep South in the 1960s (as in *To Kill a Mockingbird*), go whale-hunting aboard a 19th-century ship (see: *Moby Dick*), or explore the galaxy beyond our solar system (read: *The Hitchhiker's Guide to the Galaxy*)?

Reading a book is like opening a hidden back door into someone else's brain and climbing inside. You literally see out through their eyes, feel what they feel, and think their thoughts. It's utterly immersive and unlike any other experience in the world. A 2006 study[4] even showed, in certain cases, that your brain can't tell the difference between reading about an experience and *actually experiencing it*. (I regularly disappear into books, my mind stepping through the portal of the pages while my body stays still, so I have suspected this from a young age.)

It also exposes you to myriad kinds of writing styles, as long as you don't stay in the same lane. And, once you find someone whose style you'd love to emulate, you can read everything they've written and absorb their craft.

Finally, nothing teaches you about storytelling more than simply reading stories themselves. And storytelling is *everything* when we talk about successful content writing.

By the way, at this point, if you're wondering why I'm trying to convince you to read when you're clearly already

---

[4] Annie Murphy Paul. (2012, March.). "Your Brain on Fiction." The New York Times.
https://www.nytimes.com/2012/03/18/opinion/sunday/the-neuroscience-of-your-brain-on-fiction.html

a reader (a side-effect of being a writer, or vice-versa), let me elaborate on that:

Don't just *read*. Commit to reading something, anything, every single day of your life.

And don't just passively absorb the text. Think about what you're reading critically. Notice how the writer puts sentences together. Look at how they structure their ideas. Taste the unique flavor of the words they use (or, if they're not very good, note the blandness and ask yourself WHY it's bland).

Don't just read *some* things either. Read everything. I'm not limiting you to books, here, although that's a great place to start. (Hot tip: Reading at least one page of a book every day is a great way to read more books in general.)

Read news articles from all kinds of sources, both totally objective and horrifically biased, fact and opinion, and weigh them against each other. Read blog posts. Read emails, including the salesy ones, and quantify why they're successful (or not). Read ads—do they make you want to click? *Why?* While you're at it, read billboards. Read magazines. Read the back of the cereal box. Read the marketing copy on product packaging. Read your tube of toothpaste and your bag of coffee beans.

It all counts, as long as you're critical about what you read. And, I'll argue, sneak in a good book or three from various genres and diverse authors to round out your palette.

Luckily, as Stephen King said, "Books are a uniquely portable magic." They're just plain easy to tote around, whether you carry a paperback in your bag or sneak your phone out of your back pocket to read on an app. This leaves you zero excuses for NOT reading, but that shouldn't bother you. Your writing education awaits.

Books ARE A uniquely PORTABLE magic
-Stephen King

2. Shove Past the Blank Page with AI

As a writer, you probably already write every day; you have ongoing projects for clients, one-off pieces for blogs and guest blogs, and maybe even a magnum opus, like a book, on tap at every moment.

You don't need some author telling you to cultivate a writing habit—writing is your job, so there's no "habit" involved. It's what you DO.

That said, till AI and generative language as good as GPT-3 and what's coming next came on the scene, the blank page used to be the **hardest thing to face on the planet.** Listen. It's more daunting than just about anything, including steep drops from cliffs, hairy spiders, the darkest corners of abandoned rooms, slithery snakes, public speaking to groups of 10,000s of strangers, crazed Stephen-King-IT-style clowns, heck, even getting a root canal may seem simple by comparison.

That blank page holds so many frightening possibilities. Ones where your words get all tangled and muddled, where you can't hold onto the thread of your story or purpose, when the pressure to begin, and begin *well*, is too much to shoulder.

It *used* to be we had no antigen for this grave strait of the blank page syndrome.

But now, we do.

AI can BE the blank slate replacement for us!

In Chapter 2, you'll see me use ChatGPT to help me form the basis of an email. In Chapter 3, you'll see me use it to form tweets and get some basic thoughts written down. In Chapter 4, I use Content at Scale to generate an entire, 2,500w blog! Listen—we are now living in times where AI can, and I might add *should,* replace the blank slate. Content writers: you no longer have to suffer through writing alone in a terrifying situation where *it's just you and that blank Word Doc* any longer. Goodbye. Human-only writing is the Stone Age.

If your first draft with AI sucks, that's okay, even expected! (There's a "Rerun" button in Content at Scale just for that icky first draft stage you might want to retry.) As you gain experience, you'll find great writing happens not in the moment of creation, but rather in the **edits**. That's even *more* true now, since I'm helping the team at Content at Scale launch widescale the idea of an **AIO writer** (a human that optimizes—**O**—the AI output) using my C.R.A.F.T. framework (explained in Chapter 4). The important thing is to get something down on the page, and use AI to dramatically speed up the process of *getting words out with and for you.* Because—that's moldable clay you can work with. You can't shape greatness from thin air. Just get the words down, one at a time, and go from there.

Want to see the AI tool I use and love in my own writing process? contenthacker.com/ai

3. Invest in Yourself

You'll never stop learning to be a better writer, so why not put your money where your skill lies?

Embracing this growth path must include investments, and not just monetary ones.

You need to spend time reading and absorbing great AND terrible writing. And mediocre writing. And everything in-between.

You need to spend money to advance your skills when the time is right. This might involve taking writing courses for a brush-up, learning a new writing format (like writing ads or conversion copy if you've mainly focused on blogs), purchasing books that teach you writing skills (like this one!), or even investing in coaching or mentorship.

Investing in this learning journey will make it richer. And, by default, you'll become an even better writer than you believed you could be.

Find Your High-Performing Content Writing Zone

Once you've made some mindset adjustments, once you've cultivated some great foundational writing habits, it's time to dive further into the headspace of a high-performing content writer. This involves motivation, your unique writing preferences/habits, and your environment.

1. What Motivates YOU?

Motivation is intensely personal. What motivates me to work hard, to put my nose to my keyboard and write great content, might not be what motivates you.

For example, perhaps the end user—the target audience you're writing to—drives your motivation. Your content can and should help them in some way, so you focus on that. You aim for excellence because you're helping real people with real problems.

Or, maybe your motivation is building up your skills to advance in your career. Maybe it's impressing your client. Perhaps it's the paycheck (a very common, human motivation).

Whatever your motivation source, focus on it and construct your goals around it. Don't "borrow" motivation from other people. You might find that it will fit awkwardly once you try it on, like a shoe that's two sizes too big. Instead, focus on what lights YOUR fire, what gives you meaning and purpose in your work. This is key to finding your very own high-performing content writing headspace.

2. Practice Personal Daily Affirmations

Let's circle back to those pesky negative thoughts we addressed earlier.

What's a good way to reframe your thinking and fight back against your inner bully?

The answer: Create affirmations for yourself based on your identity and values, and repeat those daily in place of your regular, negative patterns of thinking.

If you're skeptical of this strategy—maybe you're thinking "Surely my thoughts don't have an effect big enough to matter?"—let me throw some convincing numbers at you.

Did you know, for instance, that an optimistic frame of mind is directly linked to an 11-15% longer life span, on average?[5] **Positive thinking can literally lengthen your life**.

It also has the power to help you navigate life's difficulties with more grace, agility, and resilience. That means you'll grow more, too.

How do you feel when someone in your life cheers you on, encourages you, and gives you pep talks? You feel *good*, right? You feel emboldened to take risks and try hard things. Now imagine if YOU were your best cheerleader. What might you have the power to conquer?

As a naturally negative person, putting this into practice changed my life. Now, my daily affirmations serve as my "compass" that points me in the direction of positivity and growth versus negativity and stagnation.

For example, my affirmations align with my values, how I want to react to situations, and the goals I hope to achieve. And, this goes without saying, but all of them are framed positively.

Examples:

- I am confident in my ability to make progress. (happiness/self-acceptance)
- I create content that encourages and educates on a grand scale. (motivation and inspiration)
- My family and children come first, and always get my best. (family/relationships)

---

[5] Lewina O. Lee, Peter James, & Emily S. Zevon. (2019, Aug. 19). "Optimisim is associated with exceptional longevity in 2 epidemiologic cohorts of men and women." PNAS. https://www.pnas.org/doi/10.1073/pnas.1900712116

- I take setbacks well and am quick to bounce back. (growth & success)

Read about my daily personal affirmations, a key component of my morning routine, and learn how to build your own: **contenthacker.com/affirmations**

3. Emulate Your Favorite Writer's Habits

Most writers have writing heroes. Famous authors, successful bloggers, journalists, copywriters, you name it—they all count. These are creators who have a unique style and voice, and whose writing grabs people. They're the writers you aspire to be.

Think of the one you admire most, the one whose style you love and want to emulate (albeit in your unique way). Then do a deep dive to discover that writer's writing habits. How do they start each work day? How many breaks do they take? What do they eat for breakfast? What do they read for inspiration? Where do they do the brunt of their writing?

Take inspiration from some of it or all of it—your choice—and incorporate it into your writing routine.

Let's say your literary hero is Ursula Le Guin, the celebrated sci-fi writer. She famously laid out her deceptively simple routine in an interview.[6] Studying this routine offers some ideas for your habits. For instance, Le Guin woke up before dawn every day but

---

[6] Open Culture. (2019, Jan.). "Ursula K. Le Guin's Daily Routine: The Discipline That Fueled Her Imagination."
https://www.openculture.com/2019/01/ursula-k-le-guins-daily-routine-the-discipline-that-fueled-her-imagination.html

didn't immediately sit down to write. She gave herself space to dream (e.g. "wake up and lie there and think") as well as time to eat a hearty breakfast. Then she blocked out five-ish hours for writing, the brunt of her workday, with no breaks in between.

> 5:30 a.m.—wake up and lie there and think.
>
> 6:15 a.m.—get up and eat breakfast (lots).
>
> 7:15 a.m.—get to work writing, writing, writing.
>
> Noon—lunch.
>
> 1:00-3:00 p.m.—reading, music.
>
> 3:00-5:00 p.m.—correspondence, maybe house cleaning.
>
> 5:00-8:00 p.m.—make dinner and eat it.
>
> After 8:00 p.m.—I tend to be very stupid and we won't talk about this.

Le Guin's understated but effective writing routine. She won dozens of awards during her lifetime, including the Newbery Medal.

I. Love. This! It follows a natural pattern for building up the ante to creativity, acting on that creativity, and then decompressing. My day, in fact, looks oddly similar to this. Minus the 5:30 a.m. part. My bad habit that we won't talk about is a little too much Netflix bingeing at night. It's how I… *decompress* from a day of focused, high-energy writing, thinking, and business strategy in my busy roles as VP of Marketing at Content at Scale, and coach on the side at Content Hacker. (Add in a newborn in the house. He's nearing one year old now, and he's taught me a lot. I've never had better focus when I do sit down for an hour of work! Oddly, his presence inspires *more* and *better* focus. Because I know I have only so many hours in my day.)

Maybe you find this routine inspiring, or maybe you think it would never work for you. That's okay. The point is to find a routine that appeals to you and *try out* parts of it. Think of it as a science experiment. You might find new habits that elevate your writing, while others fall by the wayside. The point is to break out of your same-old, same-old mindset and hone your routine until you feel like it functions beautifully for your life and your work. (And, it will probably evolve with you as you grow, so don't be afraid to shake things up.)

4. Stack New Writing Habits One By One

Emulating your favorite writers is a great idea, but one to take lightly. Don't just blindly jump into a brand-new writing routine, completely swapping out your old habits for new ones. That isn't sustainable. You'll just get overwhelmed and quit before you see any benefits from such a dramatic change.

Instead, focus on one swap in your routine at a time. For example, try waking up every day at 5:30 a.m. instead of your usual 7:30. Don't change anything else about your routine. Keep this swap going until it feels natural and you can understand how it works for you. If it's not serving you, abandon it. If, on the other hand, you find yourself enjoying your extra two morning hours and feel more productive once you do start working, you know that habit swap is worth keeping.

Remember what science says about forming new habits: It takes *at least* two months before any fresh behavior becomes automatic. That is, that's when the habit starts to feel less hard and more natural. But—it doesn't necessarily mean the habit is cemented in your life. Researchers at University College London found that new habit formation could take as long as 254 days—about three-quarters of a year.[7]

That's why I recommend implementing one new writing habit at a time, stacking them as you go. You'll give yourself time to adjust, experiment, tweak, and ultimately improve your routine so it works for you, not against you.

5. Find the Right Writing Cave, Nook, Spot, Room, Chair, Etc.

Often, *where* you write matters just as much as how. If you're sitting in an uncomfortable seat with bad lighting and the TV blaring in the background, how much writing will you get done versus sitting in an ergonomic, comfy seat with natural light and nothing but the sound of birdsong as your accompaniment?

There's no comparison, in my estimation. Your writing environment will affect your work just as much as your confidence.

---

[7] James Clear. (n.d.). "How Long Does it Actually Take to Form a New Habit? (Backed by Science)." https://jamesclear.com/new-habit

Granted, plenty of people do excellent work in stressful surroundings. But imagine how much better that work could have been if those surroundings instead cultivated peace and productivity. It could mean the difference between "good" or "great," or the fine line where "great" crosses over into "*incredible*."

All that is to say: Don't ignore your work environment when you're trying to get into a high-performing headspace. Find the elements that give you peace, comfort, productivity, and motivation— whatever you can control, make it work for your writing needs.

That could be as simple as working next to a bright window versus hunching over your computer in a dark corner. It could mean putting on headphones and listening to ambient sounds if the room around you is unavoidably noisy. It could mean switching out your desk chair for one that supports your lower back. It could even mean getting up from your usual spot and seeking out a better one elsewhere, like in a coffee shop or a library.

Remember: You're worth it, and so is your work.

For my best tips on setting up a writing space/office, including product recommendations and productivity tips, read my Ergonomic Home Office Guide:
contenthacker.com/ergonomic-home-office-guide

Always Write with the Ingredients You Need for Excellent, Results-Earning Content

The last piece of getting in the right headspace for writing is KNOWING what excellent content looks like and writing to those standards every time. These are the three ingredients that, when mixed to perfection, produce incredible, results-getting content.

1. Care

Point blank, great writers put great care into their work: care for the audience and care for the client/brand.

In other words, you need to give a crap. You need to be thinking about who the content is for, how it will help them, AND how the content will help the client/brand advance in their goals.

If you don't care about the quality of your work, you might not be in the right profession. Great writers CARE and care deeply. Bonus: this will safeguard you against being fully replaced by AI. Because with AI writing tools like Content at Scale, *millions* of careless, non-strategic content writers will now be eliminated.

To see Content at Scale in action, with a full (free!) video tutorial from yours truly to help you step into the new zone of AI writing without feeling overwhelmed, go to: **contenthacker.com/ai**

2. Expertise

Are you an expert on the topics you're writing about?

You have to walk your talk. You must have real expertise, whether you've earned that knowledge through experience or education.

Attempting to write on a topic with no expertise is a disaster-in-waiting. Sure, research all you want, but you'll never sound like a natural expert without the gravitas of experience/education behind your words. That's because true experts have insider knowledge about their industry and topics. They share stories that underline their experience and showcase their depth of wisdom. They know where to look for great stats to add beef to any argument because they have their ear to the ground on new industry research. And they rarely regurgitate overused information or cliché tips because they've seen it all.

Without expertise, your audience will find zero value in your content. And that is the polar opposite of what you want.

3. Optimization

Make no mistake: Unoptimized content fails.

No matter the platform, you MUST optimize your content to be read—whether we're talking about Google's crawlers or people scrolling through their social feeds.

For blogs, if rankings are your goal, you must optimize with SEO. That includes keywords, keyword placement, content quality, content depth and breadth, and answering the questions users have when they search for your keyword.

For social media, you must optimize your posts for engagement, i.e., to get read. Use of storytelling, persuasion, links, hashtags, CTAs—all of this is vital to get right for a post to bring you results, whether you're looking for increased brand awareness or new leads.

Even YouTube videos need written optimization in places like the title and description.

Unoptimized content will fall into the deep cracks of internet obscurity, even if it's fantastic stuff. Don't let this happen to your content. (Thankfully, we'll cover optimization for every type of content in this guide. I'd never lead you up the mountain with no map!)

Speaking of optimization, we need to have a conversation about the gorilla in the room: AI. And we're going to talk about a *new* way to optimize: a little something I call **AIO.**

A Note About AI (Artificial Intelligence) Writing Tools

In select sections of this book, you'll find advice and tips on how to use AI writing tools to speed up and streamline your writing process.

Why?

I'll be the first to admit that I haven't always been the biggest fan of AI in content. Up until 2022, the tools and technology available (options like Jasper, HyperWrite, and even ChatGPT) just didn't measure up to my standards. The writing output from these tools was riddled with problems:

1. **Fluffy writing**. This is when you write a paragraph when a single sentence would

suffice. The output from AI writing tools has historically been stuffed with fluff, so using it in a blog would require a full rewrite.

2. **No personality or story**. An AI writing tool doesn't have your memories or experience at its disposal. All of that is locked up in your brain, and only YOU can tell it.

3. **No factual accuracy**. AI tools are notorious bullsh!tters. Inaccurate data is one of the biggest problems I see.

4. **Overwhelming to use**. For example, the Jasper interface throws dozens and dozens of templates at you—for writing frameworks, outlines, and types of content. In HyperWrite, you give the tool a bit of guidance, and then you're left staring at the dreaded blinking cursor, wondering what to do next.

5. **Zero focus on long-form content**. Neither of the top tools focuses on long-form. At most, HyperWrite and Jasper will each produce about 500 words, max, before petering out. This matters, a LOT, because long-form content is the real authority builder. At Content Hacker, we did a study on this that proved how much more ROI it produces than short-form content. ***Read the study here: contenthacker.com/content-length***

So, it's safe to say I have been healthily skeptical of AI content since the beginning. That's why what happened next is so mind-blowing.

I finally found an AI writing tool that puts my mind at ease.

All of those problems I listed above? This one doesn't have them.

It's called **Content at Scale**. *Learn more about this incredible tool here: contenthacker.com/best-ai-tool*

Content at Scale is the first tool I've seen that addresses the major issues that have stopped me from investing in AI content creation.

1. **It's original**. Originality detectors can't tell that the content is bot-written. Zero flags! That's ultra-important because Google considers automatically-generated content created solely for search engines, with no human intervention, spam. ***Read about Google's stance here: contenthacker.com/blog-writing-ai***

2. **It passes Copyscape**. Content at Scale has a trusted plagiarism detector **built into** their tool—and the content this AI writer creates passes with flying colors.

3. **The content is human-like**. This is the first tool I've seen that can produce long-form content—posts as long as 2,500-3,000 words!—on par with an expert SEO writer. It's well-written with flow and value, and hardly any fluff.

4. **The content is correctly keyword-optimized**. So many writers struggle with keyword optimization. The fact that this tool

knocks it out of the park is incredible. Enter the keyword you want your blog to rank for, and it will create properly-optimized content AND a list of related keywords, plus an on-page SEO checklist.

5. **It integrates with WordPress**. With a few clicks, your posts will automatically show up in your WordPress backend.

This tool is why I'm diving into AI content creation with no regrets. It's why I'm now recommending it as part of YOUR writing process, too.

Because remember:

AI content creation is blowing up—disrupting industries and replacing human writers.

It's no longer just a scary-sounding, sci-fi prediction that marketers are making. *It's real.*

- Jasper.ai, a popular AI writing tool, just hit a $1.5 billion valuation in 2022.[8]

- ChatGPT is blowing minds with its abilities and use cases—content planning, topic generation, outlining, drafting, and even recipe writing are all possible with this AI. In just five days after its launch, it gained 1 million users.[9]

---

[8] Christine Hall & Haje Jan Kamps. (2022, Oct. 18). "Daily Crunch: AI content developer Jasper now valued at $1.5B following capital infusion." TechCrunch. https://techcrunch.com/2022/10/18/daily-crunch-ai-content-developer-jasper-now-valued-at-1-7b-following-capital-infusion/

[9] Steve Mollman. (2022, Dec. 9). "ChatGPT gained 1 million users in under a week. Here's why the AI chatbot is primed to disrupt search as

- The technology of the top AI writing tools—ChatGPT, Jasper, Hyperwrite—all can replace a low-level human content writer, guide a non-native one to become high quality in seconds, and help with the content ideation and strategy process.

No matter how we may feel about it, AI writing software is here to stay. That means we can either learn and adapt or slowly die.

However, the *way* you use AI writing technology matters —a LOT.

AI Writing Software Is NOTHING Without Human Expertise Behind It

You may be wondering what the point of this handbook is if you can just go out, purchase an AI writing tool, and let it write your content for you.

Short answer: **You can't actually do that**. Not if you want results from your content.

Never, ever use an AI writing tool to pump out massive quantities of content that has never seen the human touch.

Content without your unique fingerprints on it WILL NOT bring results.

Instead, use AI to do a lot of the initial outlining, drafting, and gruntwork. (Especially if you're writing long-form SEO content, which you'll learn how to create in Chapter 3.)

---

we know it." Yahoo! https://www.yahoo.com/video/chatgpt-gained-1-million-followers-224523258.html

Then, get inside the AI's draft and start tinkering.

Edit, refine, rearrange, tweak, delete, and add on. Add personal stories—from you or your clients. Add unique turns of phrases and a distinct writing style. Add high-quality links to sources that support your points. Add life, color, vigor, and that dash of emotion that can only come from a human pen.

Do you see what I'm getting at, here?

Before you can enlist an AI writing tool to streamline your writing process, you need to know what the heck you're doing. You need to *have* a process in the first place!

Your expertise must drive the tool—not the other way around.

You need the knowledge and skill to write profitable content in all shapes and forms: emails. Social media posts. Long-form SEO blogs. Sales pages and landing pages.

You need to have the skill to switch up your writing style depending on the brand you're writing for.

You have to know how to infuse that style into any type of content.

You must know how to target an audience and speak to a specific persona in your content writing.

You must understand how to write persuasive copy that hooks a reader and drives them to act—whether that means clicking a link, downloading a lead magnet, or making a purchase.

You need the ability to properly structure and format content to reach specific goals, whether you're looking for search engine rankings, conversions, or engagement.

If you attempt to use an AI tool to create content without any of the above skills or expertise... If you create AI content without touching it... That content will be:

- Bland.
- Boring.
- Lifeless.
- Targeted to *no one.*
- Helpful for *no one.*
- Unoriginal.
- Unrecognizable (any average Joe Schmo could have written it).

What will happen as a result?

- Your audience won't read it. It might even confuse them if your content is usually suffused with a distinct voice and style.
- It won't rank in Google—and you might even get penalized for it.
- You won't earn conversions from it.
- That content will act as a dead weight rather than a vehicle for growth.

That's why this is so important. That's why this handbook exists. You can't expect to drive a car without first getting in-depth instruction and practice. **The same principle applies to content writing—and using AI writing tools.**

So, learn the skills first. (Thankfully, you're well on your way with this book in your hands.) Get exceptionally good at writing content. THEN, when you add AI tools like Content at Scale to the mix, you'll be *unstoppable*.

Ready to Rock… and Write?

With all that out of the way, it's time to move forward. Armed with a fresh mindset, a few new writing habits, and exactly what you need to give yourself the best chance possible at creating amazing content, we can dive straight into the how-to parts of this handbook.

In the chapters ahead, I'll teach you exactly how to craft these types of content in ways that will produce the results you want:

1. Email Writing
2. Social Media Writing
3. SEO Blog Writing
4. Sales Page Writing
5. Writing for YouTube

PLUS a special AI writing tutorial for your SEO blog production to get it to go *5-10x faster.*

And, at the end of each chapter, you'll find the exact outlines I give my writers at Content Hacker. These produce incredible content for us, the kind that gets rankings, reads, engagement, leads, and sales.

If you're ready to learn all the nitty gritty details of effective content writing, it's time to dive in head-first. Onward!

Chapter 2:

Email Writing

Email writing truly is an art form.

It's a delicate blend of engaging, persuading, and educating. A balancing act of giving value while also promoting your brand. You must know your audience intimately to get the proportions right. And, embedded into every email you send, you need that shiny golden nugget of value at the center.

The result of sending consistent, high-quality emails is worth the effort. Out of all the content types, emails get the highest ROI (return on investment) by far—a staggering $42 back for every dollar you spend.[10]

Marketers in general also rate email as the top channel they use to connect with customers. But—only 18% say their competence with email is "advanced."

It's totally true; winning emails require a mix that can be hard to perfect... if you don't know the proven

---

[10] Direct Marketing Association (DMA). (2019). "Marketer email tracker." https://dma.org.uk/uploads/misc/marketers-email-tracker-2019.pdf

formulas for *writing* emails. (I'm a huge fan of writing formulas, by the way. They give you a fool-proof structure to follow, which you can jazz up with your personal stories, experience, research, and expertise. And, you can use a good formula over and over again in limitless ways. When I'm writing emails, I don't leave home without one.)

There are typically two goals when it comes to email, for entrepreneurs and brand owners. 1.) Sales, and 2.) Awareness that leads to sales (nurturing). Almost every email in the world can be put into one of these two buckets.

Hopefully, by the end of this chapter, you won't fear writing emails, but rather approach them with the confidence of the savviest and most successful email writers. Great emails go a long way toward boosting a brand's bottom line, so don't skip learning about this necessary content type.

What other types of content are best to grow a business? Find out here:
contenthacker.com/contenttypes

But First… Some Important Email Writing Tips to Remember

Before we jump into the actual writing bit, we need to go over the most important rules of thumb for writing *any* email, ever.

1. **Clarity over cleverness**: Make no mistake—a clear message is always better than a clever message. Unless you're a whiz at a wry, sarcastic, or punny writing style, attempted cleverness can often get in

the way of your readers comprehending your meaning. Obscure jokes and references must be carefully done, or not done at all.

2. **Benefits over features**: Writing with an emphasis on benefits means you're paying attention to what's important to your reader—NOT why your brand/product/service is amazing. Remember, your reader wants to know what they'll get out of your message. They want to know how it benefits **them**—so tell them.

3. **Keep your voice/tone consistent**: This is a general rule for content writing. A brand's voice must seamlessly flow across all its content. Documented brand voice guidelines are a big tool for ensuring this happens. If your brand (or your client's brand) doesn't have any, comb through their various channels and pinpoint how they present themselves so you can emulate that voice correctly inside their emails.

   - *Download an example of brand voice guidelines (our very own at Content Hacker!):* **contenthacker.com/brand-style-guidelines**
   - *Get a template to work through your brand style:* **contenthacker.com/brandworksheet**

4. **Speak directly to the reader**: In 99.9% of cases, you need to write in the second-person perspective; i.e., address the reader directly with "you" and "your." Even if your brand voice is formal and scientific, you want to ensure you're speaking TO your audience, not AT them. Case in point: Note the difference between these two sentences. Which one

sounds stuffy and distanced, and which one sounds warm and direct?

- *"To write a good email, you need to stay reader-focused."* (Second-person perspective)
- *"To write a good email, one must stay focused on the reader."* (Third-person perspective)

5. **Stay relevant**: Staying relevant doesn't just mean staying on-topic; it also means you have your finger on the pulse of what your audience cares about (and what they *don't* care about). Emails are not the time to dump your opinions and ramblings on your subscribers. Stick to the topic you've promised in your email headline and adhere to your **goals** for the email. Save your opinionated blabs for off-the-cuff social media, like Instagram Stories (and even then, try to stay relevant to your audience's concerns and pain points).

With that out of the way, we can jump straight to the major elements you need to include in every email, no matter the type.

The Essential Elements of Email Writing, Broken Down

I don't care what kind of email you're writing—every one of them needs four elemental pieces to work. In short, every email needs a headline, at least one image, a hook, and a link/CTA (call-to-action).

Let's break them down one by one and discuss how each one pulls its weight.

1. Headline

Your email headline is the crowning jewel of your entire email. It serves dual purposes: 1.) It sets the tone for the message you'll convey, and 2.) It entices the reader to open your email.

Neglect your headline, and you won't get any opens, let alone clicks inside your email, which is the entire point. And, don't forget that your email headline will be first seen among a bevy of competing headlines inside users' inboxes (sometimes even alongside ads). You want it to stand out. You *don't* want it to get lost jockeying for position amid a sea of other duds.

Rifle Paper Co.	Launching Tomorrow: New Swim! Mark Your Calendars
West Elm	Our Floating Lines Metal Rails comes highly recommended *Plus, 1,000s of styles on SALE up to 70% off! Come back and take a
Thrive Cosmetics	[Ad] $10 Off - Our Most Popular Set - Elevate your look in under 5 minutes with this perfect eye-enhancing makeup set. Save $10
Paula's Choice®	[Ad] 20% Off Site + Ships Free - Shop 20% Off the Entire Site with Free Shipping on All Orders. Glow Your Way

Your email headline will compete against others inside the average email inbox—including ad headlines. Make sure it stands out if you want to encourage opens.

Crafting email headlines is truly something you'll get better at with practice and patience. If you struggle, it helps to review past headlines you've crafted and the corresponding open rates on those emails. Which emails were successful? How were those headlines more engaging? Learn from your past mistakes and wins to write better email headlines in the future.

Perhaps one of the best tips for writing an engaging email headline is to only promise exactly what's inside your email. Don't go over the top and build up your reader's expectations too much—that will only lead to deflated hopes when they read your email content and discover you aren't delivering. That *also* leads to depleted trust in your brand.

For example, if you write a headline like, "Open this email to discover the secret to $1,000,000 content"—and the inside of your email doesn't offer any valuable information, but only directs the reader to buy your course… *Whoosh*. That's the sound of the air escaping from the giant, hope-filled balloon your reader is clutching. On top of that, their radar for slimy sales pitches will be beeping like crazy. They'll immediately click out of your email and delete it, which is the equivalent of backing away from you slowly with shifty eyes. They don't like the feeling that email gave them, and now they just want to be far, far away from you.

It all starts with your email headline. So: Be honest. Don't over-promise. (Email headline rule #1.)

At the same time, DO use sparkling language to make your headline pop. Dig into your trove of adjectives and strong verbs. Make your headline sing. For example, let's compare a lackluster headline to one that positively shimmers with delightfulness.

Lackluster headline: *"Upgrade your phone with a new stylish and durable case."* (From a brand selling iPhone accessories.)

Luster-y headline: *"What's Poppin' T-Shirt Wise?"* + bonus preview text: *"These tees are a-trending."* (From a brand selling graphic t-shirts.)

Do you see the differences between these two headlines? The effective one uses creative language to build interest. It focuses on WHY the reader should care ("Lots of other people like the tees in this email!") The ineffective one is boring at best and doesn't give the reader any impetus to click. Who cares if your phone cases are stylish and durable—convince me how/why that will help me in my day-to-day life! Let's look at how we could rewrite that headline to be more effective:

Lackluster headline, rewritten: *"Protect your phone from fumbles and spills with style."*

Do you see how we converted the features-heavy language (emphasis on the product, not the customer) and turned it around? Now it shines a light on WHY the reader might benefit from a "new stylish and durable case"—to protect their phone from life's mishaps while keeping their style intact.

Hyper-focusing on your reader/customer is how you arrive at a good headline that will appeal to them. (Email headline rule #2.) Think of how your email content benefits them, then distill that into one line. Boom. That's your headline.

AI Email Writing: Best Practices for Using ChatGPT for Email Copy

Email outlining is an excellent use for ChatGPT—in fact, it's one of my favorites out of all the uses I've played around with in ChatGPT. Using AI to help you with email copy ideation will jumpstart your creative thinking process quite a bit, and is better by far than starting with a blank slate. Use tools like ChatGPT and Jasper to write solid email headlines and even form the base of your email copy.

I asked ChatGPT to help me write a headline and email for a new upcoming course featuring AI writing. Here's what it did:

The important thing to know about using ChatGPT or Jasper to write emails is that you'll often need to ask it to rewrite. See how I asked it to "**rewrite that to be a better, shorter headline**"? It's that simple to regenerate something better. This part is foundational to good output. Remember that AI writing tools are still *learning*, and we as humans can teach them and steer them in the direction of giving us the output we want.

I then asked it to help me write the base of an email itself. This email isn't bad. I wouldn't copy and paste it and send it to my list—you'll still need a writer involved. We have a lot of work to do to make it more personal and targeted to the list *and* the offer, but, this is a pretty decent start:

2. Image(s)

In every type of content, including emails, a good visual will speak a thousand words. That's because humans are naturally drawn to pictures and can both see and process them lightning-fast. Studies show how visually-oriented people truly are. For instance, did you know that our brains are wired to process visuals **60,000 times faster** than text? Added to that, the human brain is capable of processing entire images in as little as 13 milliseconds.[11]

---

[11] Anne Trafton. (2014, Jan.). "In the blink of an eye: MIT neuroscientists find the brain can identify images seen for as little as 13 milliseconds." MIT News. https://news.mit.edu/2014/in-the-blink-of-an-eye-0116

We're programmed to be visually oriented and can understand the contents of a picture in mere fractions of a second. So it makes sense that adding images to content—even email content—makes them instantly more engaging to our eyes.

That's why I recommend adding at least one image to all of your emails.

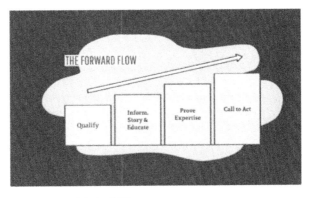

Hi [FIRST NAME GOES HERE],

At a mind-blowing 79%, the biggest goal people want to achieve through content marketing is **to generate more high-quality leads**.

But does your skin crawl when you hear the term 'lead generation funnel'?

You're **not** alone.

A Content Hacker email with a single image. At least one good image inside your email can speak a thousand words, adding depth to your message.

3. Hook

Every good email needs an attention-grabber, or hook. Your hook plays multiple roles, including engaging your reader's interest/curiosity, giving them something to relate to, or eliciting an emotional response (and, an excellent hook can do one of these things or all of these things).

Here are a few examples of hooks that worked for me:

Example: *"It sucked."* **Context:** This was my hook for sharing a vulnerable story about the struggle of hiring a good writer. Immediately, this makes the reader wonder, "What sucked?" and even further, "Tell me more!" It works on an emotional level to pull in people who have gone through that struggle and relate to that feeling.

Example: *"The lies society (and sometimes our own brain) tell us NEED. TO. END."* **Context**: This started a message where I shared my outrage over the myths of society that hold back my ideal clients. This hook has a strong, unwavering point of view that challenges status quo thinking. The idea that society lies to us, that our own brains lie to us regularly, is astonishing if you've never thought about it before.

As you can see, a good hook is often *emotional* in some shape or form. Your hook shouldn't mince words but share a viewpoint, a fact, or a feeling unequivocally. And, this little snippet of text should evoke some feelings from your reader (curiosity, hope, outrage, empathy, etc.).

Your hook is what gets your reader to... well... **read**, so always craft a hook to earn their interest.

4. Link/CTA

So, you've grabbed your reader's attention. You made them open your email, and you hooked them with your writing. Your message is getting absorbed and the reader feels positive about you/your brand. What now?

If you leave it there, you'll miss the opportunity to take that reader's interest and turn it into positive action. This is where the link/CTA (call-to-action) piece of your email rolls in.

Think of it like a snowball. If you keep rolling it forward through the snow, it will keep getting bigger. Similarly, if you direct your reader's attention to the action they can take after you've secured their interest, you're building on the trust you've already established.

That action = clicking your link. So always include at least one in every email you write, whether that link goes to a blog, a freebie, or a sales page.

Let's get right to it:

How to Build a Lead Generation Funnel That Doesn't Feel Slimy: Introducing The Forward Flow

Here's to being one of the GOOD marketers.

Julia McCoy

Content Hacker™

Your email link can be straightforward, as in this Content Hacker email we sent out sharing a new blog post with our audience.

Now that we have all the building blocks of effective emails, we can put them together in different ways to create every kind of email your brand needs. First up: blog (nurture) emails.

Types of Email: How to Write a Nurturing Email

This type of email is the simplest one to create. It also has the simplest purpose: to share newly-published blogs or other types of content (podcast episodes, videos, etc.) with your email list. For that reason, a lot of the content in said blog can be repurposed here.

I send out this type of email whenever a new blog goes live on our site—we recently switched to a "Weekly Best of" format, now that Content Hacker has its own podcast *and* a weekly blog. Instead of sending one blog per piece, we do a weekly recap. This way, users get a value-rich email once per week. Our open rate is 22%+ and greater, depending on the time of day I send it (mid-morning and early evening work well for us). We include a unique hook along with "Weekly Best of" in the title, so readers can get used to seeing value from us every week.

- **Example**: "Weekly Best of: How to build content effectiveness"
- *See the full email example:* **bit.ly/exampleweeklynewsletter**
- *Sign up to get these:* **contenthacker.com/subscribe**

Your schedule might look different for you depending on how often you publish. The important thing is to send the email so your subscribers (arguably some of the most invested members of your audience!) know when you have new content. Ultimately, that drives more traffic to your posts and nurtures their interest.

Need inspiration? Some great examples of nurturing emails come from Ann Handley's Total Annarchy newsletter (*annhandley.com/newsletter*), Mark Schaefer's {grow} newsletter (*businessesgrow.com/subscribe*), and Eddie Shleyner's Very Good Copy newsletter (*verygoodcopy.com*).

The key behind each of these newsletters—and the key to a good nurturing email in general—is how they continue to build on the relationship the brand initially established with the consumer (whether that consumer first found them through blog content, videos, their website, etc.).

After all, what do you think of, when you think of relationship-building? For most people, that probably includes discovering shared interests, chatting about topics you know you have in common already, and telling stories. And that's exactly what you can do in your nurture emails.

To that end, don't just share a new blog link with your email subscribers. Have a conversation about it, or start one. Talk to your readers. Tell a story. Let's look at some examples.

Ann Handley, for instance, is endlessly conversational in her emails. She asks questions and invites you to enter the discussion at every turn. In this email,[12] the subject line starts, "Is jargon always bad?"

Source: *Ogit*

Welcome to the 119th issue of Total Annarchy, a fortnightly newsletter by me, Ann Handley, with a focus on writing, marketing, living your best life. I'm glad you're here. If this newsletter was forwarded to you, you need your own. Subscribe here.

Boston, Sunday, August 14, 2022

That subject line. It's a layup question, isn't it?

Easy to answer "yes."

As if I just asked you "Should we protect the vulnerable?" Or "Are face tattoos a bad idea?"

Of course. Of course jargon is bad.

Or... is it always?

---

[12] Ann Handley. (2022, Aug. 14). "TA #119: Is jargon always bad?" Total Annarchy newsletter. https://archive.aweber.com/newsletter/totalannarchy/MTU0MDA3MD I=/ta-119-is-jargon-always-bad.htm

Look how many questions she fires off in this intro! I count four alone, and they're all directed at *me*—at us, the readers. It's literally like we're having a chat. This is engaging, yes, but it's also relationship-building.

Next, look at this email[13] from Mark Schaefer.

Today I bring you a few small observations on marketing that are a little too small for a full post.

Let's start with a toilet.

I was in a hotel in Madrid last month and this was on top of the toilet in my room:

I was haunted by this for two days. Why would somebody sign the top of the toilet? Who is this person? Did they make the thing? Is this a toilet influencer?

I would not count myself as a toilet expert, but I suppose I've seen my share. There seemed to be nothing unusual about this commode.

The subject line is "Seven small observations on marketing right now." And he begins by telling us a story about a toilet.

What's the thing hooking our attention, here? It's the *story*! It's the act of sharing. And throughout this whole newsletter, Mark continues this theme. He *shares* the entire

---

[13] Mark Schaefer. (2022, Oct. 3). "Seven small observations on marketing right now." {grow} Archive. https://archive.aweber.com/newsletter/totalannarchy/MTU0MDA3MD1=/ta-119-is-jargon-always-bad.htm

time—about sparks of inspiration he's had, trends he's noticed, news that intrigued him, and more. And that act of sharing draws us closer.

As you can see, nurturing means sharing. It means conversation. It means speaking to your reader on an intimate level. So don't just write, "Hey (subscriber first name), we have a new blog out this week, here you go." Instead, be conversational. Spark some interest and inspiration. Give a little more. Share a story that ties in. Your nurturing emails will go a lot further.

Want to see just how amazing email gets *after* a talented, trained writer takes over? If you're a founder, you'll want to keep reading. This example comes from one of my very own Content Hacker clients, Paul Klein over at Bizable.TV.

When we first met, he was falling severely behind on his emails and was having to rush and write each one. This wasn't good—Paul's company, Bizable.TV, was a rocket headed to the moon and just one partnership was landing him 30,000 new subscribers! So, it was important (to say the least) for him to get on top of email. Now, after I coached both him and his writer (services I offer at Content Hacker), he's ahead of his email schedule *and* incorporating high-quality copy in every email. Look at the DRAMATIC difference between his emails before and after my service, where we found and trained an expert writer for him. Personally, I am such a huge fan of his email transformation, I now read and look for Paul's ghostwritten emails in my inbox every week.

Learn more about Paul and Bizable.TV at bizable.tv

Bizable.TV's emails *before* getting a trained, expert writer involved:

Are you feeling overwhelmed, like there's never enough time to get all of your tasks done each day?

Join Teresa McCloy the creator of the REALIFE Process®, and learn how to Live from REST Not RUSH.

As a recovering workaholic who was addicted to all the latest apps, software, and best-selling books on productivity.

Teresa is passionate about helping business owners assess their habits and execute a process to take their everyday, ordinary life to something extraordinary in their REALIFE, REALWORK & REALSELF.

Join Teresa and I for this great BizableTV University Session.

→ Get 4 Time Blocks to Build your Most Productive Week in Business

Nothing but the best of the best for you!

To your success-

Paul Klein, Co-Founder, BizableTV

You're receiving this email and updates because you signed up to our email list.

If it's too much or too much Unsubscribe or update the Update your profile here.

For Bizable, support or issues of all our content, products or services you are allowing each for us to help. You'll find that this stuff is good.

You can keep your name and this email list with from these emails. Share them with us to see. Share from on: The BizableTV Letter

Try the The BizableTV Podcast is available on iTunes, Amazon Alexa, Google, IHeart Radio and Spotify.

Bizable Marketing, LLC, dba BizableTV™ 1441 New Highway 96 W, ste 2 - 8150, Franklin, TN 37064

Bizable.TV's emails *after* getting a trained, expert writer:

Becoming an entrepreneur entails that you step off into the precipice of the unknown, yet it can be a terrifying experience, fraught with unforeseen perils and inherent loneliness.

Doubt, fear, and overthinking can start to take hold, paralyzing your ability to think and act in the present moment.

Fear is a universal aspect of the human condition, but it does not have to be the enemy.

When you choose to reexamine your relationship with fear – or with any problems that may arise – you start to focus on what you can control.

In today's episode of BizableTV, **Mental Performance Coach & Speaker, Lauren Johnson** explains how you can develop the necessary mental skills that will make you invincible and adaptable.

Through her experience with athletics, she illustrates the ways her identity has been shaped by belief and action.

Belief, in turn, is shaped by identity and action.

It can be difficult to shift your paradigm when it is being clouded by blind spots and intrusive emotions.

However, the power to choose your response, beginning with the separation of truth from feelings, can alter the demarcation of power.

Adversity is inevitable – it's the response that determines which outcomes you receive.

Key takeaways from today's episode:

- 0:50 – Introducing Lauren Johnson, a mental performance coach and speaker who specializes in performance psychology.
- 3:42 – How growth comes from learning to redefine our relationship with the problem.
- 6:14 – Get advice for those dealing with uncertainty or negative feedback.
- 9:35 – How focusing on the present in order to manage fear.
- 16:28 – Why Lauren's epiphany while she was working at **Starbucks** was a breakthrough.
- 20:22 – How Lauren's work with the **New York Yankees,** was able to help a player cast away limiting beliefs.
- 26:40 – Why finding someone you trust to elicit honest feedback and identify blind spots is important.
- 32:15 – How shifting your mindset to navigate negativity to quickly make progress.

Watch Now

Nothing but the best of the best for you!

To your success-

Paul Klein

Co-Founder, BizableTV

A Cool Resource For You

My friend Teresa McCloy has a great new book called **Do What Matters** and you can **get the Kindle version for only $0.99** between September 8th - 20th.

Its a great read for this weekend, so pick it up today for $0.99.

Stop Scanning For A Second!

Ok, if you are still with me at the bottom of this email....I really do appreciate you!

I am sitting here this morning having my coffee like many of you (literally, its 9:33 am CMT), crafting this email before it goes out to you today.

I missed the week before last because we were in Dallas, TX for Podcast Movement filming a new Trailer for The Creator Revolution

We got to walk around and visit with so many interesting creative entrepreneurs, including **Dan Miller and Julia McCoy from Content Hacker.**

We also interviewed **John Lee Dumas from Entrepreneurs On Fire!**

How cool is that!

What's on my heart this morning is how to make this weekly email the most valuable to you.

I do struggle with this regularly, as you can see from the different versions over the last few months.

My question to you is this:

What format of the weekly email do you prefer?

> 1. **Do you like the weekly BizableTV episode announcements (like above for Jennifer)?**

OR

> 2. **Do you prefer business strategies and event summaries?**

Just Click Reply And Type #1 or #2

I don't want to waste your time(o:

You're the best!

Paul

PS: Also open to other ideas and of course you can always unsubscribe here

I usually send weekly emails and I promise to send you my best stuff.

If that's too much, click here Unsubscribe or you can Update your profile here

No affiliate premise, none of these articles, products, or services are affiliates and are being recommended... well, because they're good!

Do you know someone that might benefit from these emails? Have them subscribe to future emails here The BizableTV Letter.

The The BizableTV Podcast is available on iTunes, Amazon Alexa, Google IHeart Radio and Spotify

Koss Consulting LLC, dba Bizable, LLC. 1441 New Highway 96 W, ste 2 - #150, Franklin, TN 37064

Just a simple weekly digest can build massive trust with your following. At Content at Scale, we send a *rapidly-growing* email list a simple weekly roundup of all of our blogs and new content. **Here's an example of one: bit.ly/contentatscaleweeklydigestexample**

And here's what a reader, Marcos at misaias.com, said *two weeks into* our launch of the Weekly Digest:

"I love the product, but this Digest is Gold. Receiving it on Friday afternoon makes it feel like a treat!

THANK YOU, and keep coming this kind of insightful content. (Youtube videos included)

You got a faithful subscriber and affiliate marketer/promoter here."

See the value of building trust with simple emails?

Now, let's get into the specifics of how to write each part of a nurturing email that 1.) shares your newest published content or 2.) shares one of your lead magnets.

1. Headline

Re-use the headline from your blog for your email subject/headline. You can reword it a bit to make it shorter if needed. Otherwise, just copy and paste.

Examples:

- Blog headline: "How to Build a Lead Generation Funnel That Doesn't Feel Slimy: Introducing the Forward Flow"
  - Corresponding email headline: "New blog: How to build a non-slimy lead gen funnel"

- Video interview generating an email headline: "Leveraging the Power of Your Mind With Lauren Johnson" (Paul Klein)
- Email headline from the Total Annarchy newsletter: "How to write sales copy that doesn't sound like you're pitching on QVC" (Ann Handley)
- Email headline from the {grow} newsletter: "The long ugly road of measurement and influencers" (Mark Schaefer)

2. Image

Include a single image at the top of your blog. This is a great place to repurpose images from the actual blog, especially if you had any custom-designed ones. Choose one that illustrates the overall topic of your blog, or a key idea.

3. Hook

Again, repurpose from your blog! The hook here will be the first 200 words, or the   intro   section that comes before the first header. A well-written blog will have an enticing hook, so get the most mileage you can from it.

Don't forget to be conversational, here, as well. For instance, edit your blog intro to include a few more questions, or add a story related to the blog you're sharing.

Here's an example of a hook from a Content Hacker blog repurposed in the email promoting that same blog.

Blog:

How to Build a Lead Generation Funnel That Doesn't Feel Slimy: Introducing The Forward Flow

 by Julia McCoy May 24, 2022

At a mind-blowing 79%, the biggest goal people want to achieve through content marketing is to generate more high-quality leads.

But does your skin crawl when you hear the term "lead generation funnel"?

You're **not** alone.

Annoying popups. Endless upsells. Aggressive click funnels. 🏃

This can feel like the modern-day equivalent to yucky telemarketing strategies.

But effective lead generation doesn't have to be this way.

In fact, there's an even better way to bring awareness, engagement, and conversions to your digital marketing strategy.

By using an attraction-based marketing funnel.

Email:

Hi [FIRST NAME GOES HERE],

At a mind-blowing 79%, the biggest goal people want to achieve through content marketing is **to generate more high-quality leads.**

But does your skin crawl when you hear the term 'lead generation funnel'?

You're **not** alone.

Annoying popups. Endless upsells. Aggressive click funnels.

This can feel like the modern-day equivalent to yucky telemarketing strategies.

But effective lead generation doesn't have to be this way.

In fact, there's an even better way to go about bringing awareness, engagement, and conversions to your digital marketing strategy.

By using an attraction-based marketing funnel.

4. *Blog Link*

Super straightforward: Include a link to the blog you're promoting somewhere in the email. Usually, I include it near the bottom, after the hook. That way, you'll build that interest we talked about, which also means you'll have a better chance of earning a click.

Now, let's look at how all the pieces work together to create a blog (nurture) email. Here's a real-life example:

BLOG (NURTURE) EMAIL EXAMPLE

HEADLINE:

New blog: How to build a non-slimy lead gen funnel

EMAIL COPY:

I've created (and tested!) a new formula, called The Forward Flow. Today, I'm sharing it with the world.

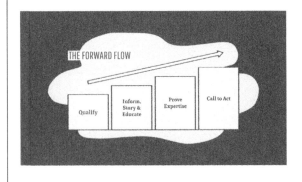

Hi [FIRST NAME GOES HERE],

At a mind-blowing 79%, the biggest goal people want to achieve through content marketing is **to generate more high-quality leads.**

But does your skin crawl when you hear the term 'lead generation funnel'?

You're **not** alone.

Annoying popups. Endless upsells. Aggressive click funnels. 🧍

This can feel like the modern-day equivalent to yucky telemarketing strategies.

But effective lead generation doesn't have to be this way.

In fact, there's an even better way to go about bringing awareness, engagement, and conversions to your digital marketing strategy.

By using an attraction-based marketing funnel.

One that's built on trust — because building trust with customers is more important now than ever before (people now trust businesses more than their own governments).

So that's great news for marketers (whether you're building a B2C or B2B lead generation funnel).

Because it means people are ready to connect with you and your brand — if you approach marketing with **authenticity**.

In this article, I'll show you how it's done.

We'll dive into:

1. How to build a (non-slimy) lead generating funnel that uses real-life content

2. My secret formula, the Forward Flow, to inject inside your sales funnels that builds trust and brings in leads

3. How to make this process repeatable while keeping it rooted in authenticity

...and more juicy marketing tips for a high-converting funnel. 💥

Let's get right to it:

How to Build a Lead Generation Funnel That Doesn't Feel Slimy: Introducing The Forward Flow

Here's to being one of the GOOD marketers,

Julia McCoy

Content Hacker™

Don't forget: We have templates that show you EXACTLY what high-ROI email copy should look like (and these templates are updated by yours truly, consistently). Get your hands on the Drive folder where I store all my writing templates here: **contenthacker.com/templates**

How to Write a "Give Value" Email

The second-simplest email to write is the "give value" email. As the name implies, this content is all about giving your audience amazing value that makes them glad they're signed up to your email list. (At Content Hacker, we've literally had people reply to thank us after sending these types of emails.) And, remember, giving value = building that coveted trust.

Generally, I like to send the "give value" email whenever we release a new freebie or download. You can also send this email to remind your followers of your cache of existing freebies and encourage downloads if they haven't done so yet. In this instance, we're going to write a "give value" email that shares a lead magnet with our audience and encourages them to download it.

1. Headline

Your lead magnet email can have the same headline as the lead magnet itself. For example, a real lead magnet on Content Hacker is called "The Profitable Content Marketer Skills Cheat Sheet." I could copy and paste this title straight onto my email headline with a few extra words to add interest, such as, "New freebie: The Profitable Content Marketer Skills Cheat Sheet."

2. Image

In most cases, you can repurpose images you've already used in blogs or across your site.

In this example lead magnet email, we used images straight from the lead magnets we were promoting. Along with adding interest, this also gives readers a little preview of what they could download.

Click to download *The Art of Writing for An Online Audience*. Includes a free look at lessons from one of our most popular Academy short courses, Unlearn Essay Writing.

Click to download *The Profitable Content Marketer Skills Cheat Sheet*. Includes a look at some of the tools and techniques we teach in-depth in our mentorship. CTS

Click to download *The SEO Content Writer's FAQ*. Includes free content from my Expert SEO Content Writer Course.

☐ You can click each book to go straight to the matching guide

3. Hook

The hook for your lead magnet email needs to get people interested in downloading what you're offering. For this reason, you should double down on the ultimate **benefits** of downloading and reading your freebies.

The best, simplest way to do this? Write a one-sentence summary of WHO the freebie is for (e.g. the audience the lead magnet targets) and WHAT it does to help them (what are the ultimate benefits? What will they learn, and how will that knowledge improve their work/lives?).

4. Link/CTA

Simple: Link directly to your lead magnet. Since your readers are already on your list, you can skip the landing page where you collect their information. Just give them the goods!

For the link text, keep it super simple and include a CTA (call-to-action) like, "Download now: [Title of freebie]" or "Click to download: [Title of lead magnet]".

Click to download The Art of Writing for An Online Audience Includes a free look at lessons from one of our most popular Academy short courses: Unlearn Essay Writing.

An example of a CTA with a link to download the lead magnet. BONUS: See how we've gently and non-pushily upsold on a matching deeper course.

Now that we've gone over all the pieces you need for a lead magnet (give value) email, let's look at a real-life example to see them all together in action.

"GIVE VALUE" EMAIL EXAMPLE

HEADLINE:

Free reading material for your long weekend

EMAIL COPY:

Hi {{ subscriber.first_name }},

Want to learn SEO, content strategy, or online writing?

We *just* updated all of our hottest guides on each of these topics with fresh content. ✹

These have been downloaded and read by thousands of marketers!

Enjoy some epic reading material this long weekend.

Click to download: The Art of Writing for An Online Audience. *Includes a free look at lessons from one of our most popular Academy short courses, Unlearn Essay Writing.*

Click to download: The Profitable Content Marketer Skills Cheat Sheet. *Includes a look at some of the tools and techniques we teach in-depth in our mentorship, CTS.*

Click to download:_The SEO Content Writer's FAQ. Includes free content from my_Expert SEO Content Writer Course.

📖 You can click each book to go straight to the matching guide:

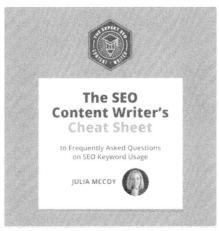

Enjoy!

Happy long weekend (& 4th, if you're in the States!),

~ Julia

Founder, Content Hacker™

How to Write a Sales (Offer) Email

Sales emails are arguably the hardest to write. You need to understand the art of persuasion, of leading a reader through their doubts, past their pain points, and ultimately to a solution (your product/service) *without* being too blunt or in-your-face. You want to gently sell, carefully nudging prospects in the right direction, banking on the trust you've already spent so much time building. You *don't* want to throw your sales pitch at them with the force of a sledgehammer. You *don't* want to make them feel like the decision to buy into your offer is anything but a brilliant idea that will advance their interests and ease that pain they're trying to solve.

How do you do all that? With a formula, my friends.

Where to Find Topics for Sales Emails

Before we hop to the formula for writing, first let's address how you come up with topics for your sales emails in the first place. Ask yourself a few key questions:

What are you selling?

How can you tie that into storytelling and sharing value?

Hot tip: I recommend mining the exact same topic areas you use for social media stories, for your sales emails. (Turn to *Chapter 4: Social Media Writing* to see what I mean.) Examples of topics to focus on:

- Interactions with ideal clients (what questions did they ask? What struggles did your brand help them overcome?)
- Vulnerable truths (failures and how your brand overcame them)
- The myths your brand dispels in your industry, about your industry
- Relating what your brand does to your industry—e.g., if you're in fitness, relate patterns of success like going to the gym regularly with patterns of success for marketing ("Consistency in marketing is like going to the gym")

Still struggling to find topics? Consider combing through your client/brand's story for nuggets you can share with your audience. There are always tiny stories within a larger story—you just need to find them. For example, in my own Content Hacker brand story, just a slice of what's mentioned includes starting from nothing, creating ugly flyers at the beginning, failing for four years out of 10, etc. All of these can be shared individually as tiny stories in sales emails to connect with readers and show them the power of our services, which are based on trials and errors in my career, which now spans over a decade.

To sum up, find ways to be relatable, to be empathetic and sympathetic, to connect with prospects deeply, to be vulnerable and real, if you want to sell with heart (and sell well) with an email.

Now, with a topic in hand, let's dive into the pieces of our formula.

1. Headline

Your sales (offer) email headline needs to be strong, undoubtedly. To do that, focus on building intrigue, here. Tap into vulnerability by mentioning hard-won lessons learned or mistakes made. These things build a whopping amount of trust when selling an offer.

Example: "What I learned from creating brands that fell FLAT"

This headline was attached to an email selling/promoting my business mentorship program, The Content Transformation System. It builds intrigue, as it makes you ask, "WHAT did she learn?" while also evoking empathy (my target audience also possibly has experienced business or career failure in their lives).

As you can see, a good headline always aims to reach out and grab the reader. If you're not appealing to their curiosity, their emotions, their empathy, or their problems, you won't accomplish that.

A strong headline is also never generic. Synonyms: boring, flat, dull, same-old, obvious, underwhelming.

To show you what I mean, here's an example of a sales headline I could have used (and other brands have used ad-nauseum, in various iterations) to sell my program.

Bad sales email headline example: "The Content Transformation System: the ONLY business program you need!"

YAWN. This line makes me want to sling back a big, fat "SO WHAT?" to the brand. It's very "Look how great we are. Let us tell you about it" and that elicits nothing but one word from me: yuck. It breaks every rule of great headline writing (remember those?) because 1.) It overpromises. 2.) It's focused on the company, not on the customer. 3.) It's also generic and unengaging. Strikes three and four.

Finally, remember to spend **time** crafting your sales email headlines. Don't go with the first line that pops into your head; instead let it simmer for a while, like a pot of stew. Let the flavors intensify. Add spice and seasoning. For me, when writing this type of copy, I might go through 20 versions before I hit the right one. Don't be afraid to tinker, to play around with words and their order. Eventually, you'll strike the right note and tone, and that headline will sing like Adele.

2. Image

Nope, we're still not neglecting images, even in sales email content. I'd wager that adding an image here is even more important than ever. After all, images speak a thousand words, and human brains process them much more quickly than text. They add additional color, interest, and engagement to your sales emails, too. I believe they're so important, 99% of my offers include a custom image for that offer.

As far as where/when to add one, keep it simple. Stick one at the top of your email with the content underneath. Keep the image relevant, and, if possible, branded. Here's how that looks in a real offer email I sent out for Content Hacker:

Headline: **What I learned from creating brands that FELL FLAT**

Product-market-fit is critical. here's why

Hi [FIRST NAME GOES HERE],

3. Hook (Story/Value)

If your headline is the mast of your sales email, the hook is your rudder. It's what will ultimately drive your email, and tells your prospect WHY they should care and WHY your solution (the product/service) is the answer.

However, always share this information through the vehicle of **story** and **value**. Tell a valuable story that relates the product/service to an undeniable benefit or positive outcome. Tie it back to the WHY behind the brand. Let's look at this in action.

In this example sales email, I start with a story. I tell you how I failed to create two successful brands after spending months of time and energy building them.

It's so cringeworthy (heartbreaking, really).

Spending months of time, energy, and money working on a business idea...

Then, it flops.

It's happened to me not once, **but twice**.

It's true...out of the seven brands I've built, two were duds.

Next, I tie the reason for that failure to a problem that many business owners face: My idea was great, and I thought the world needed it... But nobody *wanted* it.

After that, we jump into how biz owners can avoid this common issue: with my service!

But I learned...I grew...I took note:

And in both cases, **the reason for failure was identical**.

I had a 'great' idea for something the world needed!

...but nobody actually wanted.

So how can you avoid this and make sure your idea has legs?

We teach that, in the Skillset Phase of The Content Transformation System. You'll learn how to map out a product-market-fit so your offer never falls flat. Your offer *must* be based on what people need at a price they are willing to pay (not dependent on your worth).

From my story to my target audience's pain point to my offered solution, it all ties together in a neat bow. One leads to the next and then the next, like gentle drops of rain collecting in a bucket. A couple of drops on their own won't make any difference, but if it keeps sprinkling, the bucket will eventually fill up. And that's exactly what you want.

4. Link/CTA (Offer)

Here's where your actual offer comes in. This part of the email needs just as much care and attention as the other parts because the way you phrase the offer ultimately will be the deciding factor for whether your prospect opts in or not.

This can be intimidating, but don't let it be. There are a few keys to follow that will make it relatively straightforward.

First: Forget the hard sell. Phrases like "Buy now," "Limited time offer," "Act now," etc. are all spammy and create a false sense of urgency—which is NOT what you want. We're not here to pressure our audience, but rather gently nudge them in the right direction. We want them to buy, but we want them to be *wildly happy* about it because we're helping them with the product/service in a powerful way. Remember, with holistic content marketing, we've already been building their interest, trust, and loyalty with content beyond email (blogs, social media, videos, etc.). So the softer sell will be more effective than the hard sell, because at this point the hard sell is overkill—and frankly, *icky*.

Along with a soft, gentle sell, you also want to be positive when you present the offer. Selling negatively will turn people off. Examples: "This won't last forever!" or "We'd hate for you to miss out on this offer" or "You might not be ready for [product/service benefit]."

Instead, soft, positive, encouraging, and empathetic are what you should be aiming for, here. Make it feel like an invitation rather than an imperative. Here's a great example from a real email we sent: "P.S. Questions? Wanna talk strategy? Feel free to book a free call with us here."

Finally, don't forget to link directly to the sales page, application page, or enrollment page for the product/service you're selling—a good practice is to add the hyperlink to the action word or phrase in your call-to-action (e.g. "apply," "download," "enroll," "sign up," etc.).

Here's how we presented the offer in our sales email example:

Apply and see if you qualify for our 12-month mentorship, where we literally teach you THE LATERAL PATH to 7/8 figures without breaking (*see how it works in this 20 min free training*).

Once you apply, you can book a free call with us to chat about your idea + see if it will make money.

We love jumping on these zero-pressure strategy calls and answering questions about the power of The Content Transformation System and what it can do for you (apply now).

The best news is the options in this email are 100% free.

Your journey of 1,000 steps (7 figures... a business you love running... no burnout)... starts with one.

Apply now to see if you qualify for our business growth mentorship + book a free chat at the end.

Note the soft sell language: "Apply now and see if you qualify," "Book a free call," "zero pressure." We're not pushing or forcing—we're inviting.

Finally, finally, remember clarity and brevity always win versus long-winded blathering for sales emails. You want to keep it simple (second-grade reading level!—

and no, this doesn't mean dumbing things down, but rather keeping your meaning utterly clear with no fluff), direct, succinct, and scannable so quick readers get the gist of your offer in a flash.

Ready to see all the pieces of an effective sales (offer) email put together? Right this way.

SALES (OFFER) EMAIL EXAMPLE

Headline: What I learned from creating brands that FELL FLAT

Email Copy:

Product-market-fit is critical...here's why

Hi [FIRST NAME GOES HERE],

It's so cringeworthy (heartbreaking, really).

Spending months of time, energy, and money working on a business idea…

Then, it flops.

It's happened to me not once, **but twice**.

It's true…out of the seven brands I've built, two were duds.

But I learned…I grew…I took note:

And in both cases, **the reason for failure was identical**.

I had a 'great' idea for something the world needed!

…but nobody actually wanted.

So how can you avoid this and make sure your idea has legs?

We teach that, in the Skillset Phase of The Content Transformation System. You'll learn how to map out a product-market-fit so your offer never falls flat. Your offer *must* be based on what people need at a price they are willing to pay (not dependent on your worth).

Apply and see if you qualify for our 12-month mentorship, where we literally teach you THE LATERAL PATH to 7/8 figures without breaking (*see how it works in this 20 min free training*).

Once you apply, you can book a free call with us to chat about your idea + see if it will make money.

We love jumping on these zero-pressure strategy calls and answering questions about the power of The Content Transformation System and what it can do for you (apply now).

The best news is the options in this email are 100% free.

Your journey of 1,000 steps (7 figures... a business you love running... no burnout)... starts with one.

Apply now to see if you qualify for our business growth mentorship + book a free chat at the end.

Snag these amazing opportunities while you can.

Cheers to you,

Julia

Creator, Content Hacker

P.S. Want a quick, amazing free guide will help you know discover exactly how (and if) your business idea will fit in the market (lessons usually reserved for students of my coaching program)? Read my Serious Business Owner Map.

Rules for Sending Emails (What to Send & How Often)

When sending emails, I have a few rules I like to follow that help keep things consistent. These are my guidelines:

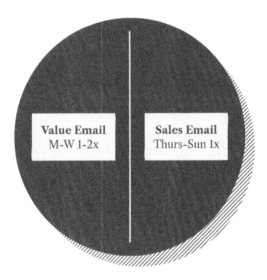

1. Send Emails Twice Weekly

Setting up a consistent schedule nurtures and converts your list. Keeping it to twice a week ensures you aren't spamming their inboxes.

Remember: If you're not doing content well and consistently, there's zero point.

On what days should you send your emails? At what times? Generally, studies have found that the best days to send emails are **Tuesday and**

Thursday.[14] These days have gotten the best email open rates across many different studies from HubSpot, GetResponse, and Intercom. As for times to send emails, this is a bit more dependent on your particular audience. A good practice is to test sending emails sometime between 10 a.m. and 2 p.m. Then, see what results you get. If they're consistently not great, try switching up your time slot and testing again.

2. Send One Value-Focused Email Monday – Wednesday

Ideally, your value-focused email will share the valuable content you post weekly (see the nurturing email outline at the end of this chapter for a quick refresher).

Write emails for your blog, your podcast, a new YouTube video, etc. At Content Hacker, we typically send two of these weekly—one corresponding to a new blog, and one for a podcast. These are short emails with a direct link to the piece of content. And, though it goes without saying, the linked content is ALWAYS valuable in and of itself. (To learn to write value-rich blog content, head to *Chapter 3: SEO Blog Writing.*)

---

[14] Melinda Bartley. (2022, June 17). "The Best Time to Send Emails to Boost Opens, Clicks, and Sales." Optinmonster. https://optinmonster.com/the-best-time-to-send-emails-heres-what-studies-show/

3. Send One Offer Email Thursday – Sunday

Save the end of the week for sending your offer email (see: *How to Write a Sales [Offer] Email* + the outline provided at the end of this chapter). Friday mornings and Saturday afternoons are a great time, as we've found at my business. Often, people are in happy and contemplative moods and more likely to read AND act on our offers if we strategically send them Friday a.m. or Saturday mid-day.

Another thing: Avoid copying and pasting your offers. Write and send a **unique** offer each time you share one (the offer itself doesn't necessarily need to be new—just the copy surrounding it). Just like you wouldn't duplicate a blog post each time you publish, you should never send duplicate emails. Write fresh copy every time an offer email goes out if you expect people to respond well.

Last but not least, for an even softer sell, always include an additional CTA for booking a free call with your brand or downloading a free guide in your offer email. If you look at the sales (offer) email example, you'll see we did just that. This helps grab people who aren't quite ready to buy but are still interested.

Your journey of 1,000 steps (7 figures... a business you love running... no burnout)... starts with one.

Apply now to see if you qualify for our business growth mentorship + book a free chat at the end.

Snag these amazing opportunities while you can.

Cheers to you,

Julia

Creator, Content Hacker

P.S. Want a quick, amazing free guide will help you know discover exactly how (and if) your business idea will fit in the market (lessons usually reserved for students of my coaching program)? Read my *Serious Business Owner Map.*

Checklist for Email Writing

- o 2x per week: Value & nurturing first (always), sales second
- o Sales offers tend to do better later in the week (and weekends); give value to start the week
- o Know your main email components and how to craft each one:
    - o Headline
    - o Image
    - o Hook
    - o Link/CTA
- o Clarity over cleverness
- o Brevity over length
- o Succinct over explain-y and fluffy
- o Some emails should give value—and nothing else (no promotional ish!)
- o Some emails should include offers—but deliver them through the vehicle of story + value

- o Just say no to the hard sell ("Buy now!"; "Act fast!")
- o The soft sell—gentle, inviting, encouraging, positive—should be your go-to
- o Send emails on a regular schedule—twice weekly is a good rule of thumb
- o Don't copy and paste email content—get original copy for each one you send

Email Writing Outlines

Nurturing Email

HEADLINE: Blog title doubles as your headline!

IMAGE: Include an image at the top of your email—repurpose from the images you've included or made for your blog!

HOOK: The first 200 words of your blog, or the intro before your first subheader, go here.

BLOG LINK: Link directly to your blog!

WHAT THIS DOES: Sends your blog to your list and nurtures your audience.

"Give Value" Email

HEADLINE: Freebie title doubles as your headline!

IMAGE: Include an image at the top of your email—repurpose from the images you've included or made for your blog!

HOOK: A one-sentence summary of WHO the freebie is for, and WHAT it does to help them. **BLOG LINK**: Link directly to your blog!

WHAT THIS DOES: Gives incredible value to the lucky people on your list! We've had "thank you so much" replies sent to these emails. You only have to send one when you create a new freebie.

Sales (Offer) Email

HEADLINE: Strong headline that builds intrigue—vulnerability and your lessons learned/mistakes made build HUGE trust when selling an offer.

IMAGE: Include an image at the top of your email—if you think of an email like any written content, and how visuals speak a thousand words—then you'll see it's important to include images. 99% of my offers include a custom image for that offer.

STORY/VALUE: Give them value and share your story (a mistake you made and learned from, why you created your method, why you do what you do).

CTA: Your offer (soft, positive, empathetic—never sell negatively or you'll turn off. Keep it positive, uplifting, and feeling like an invitation. Link directly to a sales page and application or enrollment here).

WHAT THIS DOES: Sales, baby! Creates revenue for your business.

CHAPTER 3:

Social Media Writing

Social media is absolutely bonkers these days.

More people than ever are online, over-sharing, and trying to break through the noise to get noticed.

Because there's a LOT of noise.

Just to give you an idea, over 95 million posts are published on Instagram… *daily*.[15]

Facebook has 2.91 *billion* active users worldwide.[16]

Social media users around the world make up more than 75% of the eligible population (teens and adults).[17]

Added to that, tech companies have *so much control* over who sees what in the average social media feed. Their algorithms are not tuned to equal screen time for everyone.

---

[15] Mary Lister. (2022, Jan.). "31 Mind-Boggling Instagram Stats & Facts for 2022." WordStream.
https://www.wordstream.com/blog/ws/2017/04/20/instagram-statistics
[16] Statista. (2022). "Number of monthly active Facebook users worldwide as of 2nd quarter 2022 (in millions)."
https://www.statista.com/statistics/264810/number-of-monthly-active-facebook-users-worldwide/
[17] Datareportal. (2022). "Global Social Media Statistics."
https://datareportal.com/social-media-users

Instead, certain types of posts (hello, videos) get prioritized over others based on user behavior and what they interact with most *as well as* quality.

Taking all of this into account—the amount of noise on social, finicky algorithms, and fickle user engagement—how do you learn to write social media posts that not only captivate an audience, but actually survive algorithms and get airtime?

It's a tough feat, so much so that brands spend oodles of money on social media ads just to ensure they get in front of their targets.

But what if you don't need ad spend? What if fantastic writing and well-crafted copy could do the work for you?

It's possible. How?

You guessed it—there's a formula for that.

But first, let's talk about why social media isn't your best haven for long-term success.

Content House First, Social Media Second

Before we get into the nuts and bolts of social media writing, we need to time-out for a minute.

We have to talk about WHY social media shouldn't be your platform of focus for content marketing.

Yes, it's important to know how to write effective short-form content like social posts. This is a skill that will serve you well for connecting with your audience and promoting the main content that lives *on your website*.

Those three words are the keys, here: **On. Your. Website.**

Your website is your content house, or your home base on the internet. And if it's not, it should be.

Your website, your domain, is real estate YOU own. You bought it, you paid for it, it's YOURS. You control all the content that lives on it, including its visibility.

That's not true for the content you post on social media. You don't own those platforms—Meta does (Instagram and Facebook). Elon Musk does (Twitter). Microsoft does (LinkedIn). That means all the content you post there, for free, ultimately exists at the whim of a mercurial billionaire, or a faceless board of directors, or a bunch of rich CEOs with their own agendas.

Your account on Instagram could get disabled one day for no apparent reason. Your posts could be shadowbanned (disappaer from hashtag pages, the Explore page, or from visibility in people's feeds). Elon Musk could cause Twitter to self-implode, which means your content would be GONE. And on and on.

That's why you need a content house, and why you should prioritize posting content there. Your content house is your best investment for the longevity of your content AND your online presence.

Besides websites over social media, there's one more area where I deviate from a lot of other experts in my teaching. Let's talk about it, because it directly influences the type of social media writing you'll learn from me.

Why I Teach People to Write LONG Social Media Posts & Captions

Social media posts don't have to be short. In fact, the most effective posts I've written (including captions on Instagram) have all been long by social media standards—think a few paragraphs versus one or two sentences.

Why?

LONG captions build far more TRUST no matter where you post. Long captions for Reels. Long captions for LinkedIn posts. Long captions for Facebook posts.

I've been asked…why do you teach writing length on social? *That same day*, someone in our audience reported getting a lead in their inbox from a long social media post. Length works!

At Content Hacker, we even did a study where we pitted short-form content against long-form content and tracked the results—leads, customers, and sales—over a year. The takeaways were **astounding**. Long-form content earned 62x more customers than short-form. Our long-form content earned us over $200,000 in sales. By contrast, guess how many sales we made from short-form content?

One. And that person eventually wanted (and received) a 75% refund. *Oof.*

Read more about our content length study here:
contenthacker.com/length

In my mentorship, The Content Transformation System, we go deep into long-form content being a vehicle of trust and sales. I've taught and helped several solopreneurs write social media stories that brought them leads and sales *that week.* My firm belief is that your primary real estate should be your website (your content house),[18] but to build that "road" back to your house, social media is a great endeavor. Don't forget to get your website in order and your "content house" built for long-term, exit-worthy success you can hang your hat on; but *absolutely* use social media to get known, liked, and trusted.

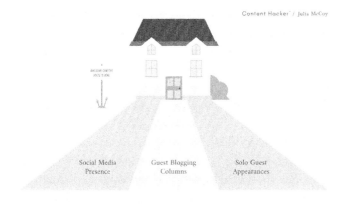

Here's how to do that—let's talk about writing for social media.

Learn more about my in-depth, hand-holding mentorship for solopreneurs and early-stage founders wanting to grow through content: **contenthacker.com/transformation**

---

[18] Contenthacker.com/content-ecosystem

Tweet Threads

Ah, the power of a good Twitter thread.

Justin Welsh, entrepreneur (justinwelsh.me) used Twitter to earn $1.2M in revenue—from 175 million impressions. He believes high-quality Twitter threads are the fastest and easiest way to pick up new followers who are interested in your expertise.

You can use ChatGPT to help you formulate some decent thread idea starters—and from there, create *better* content. The key of a good Twitter thread, Justin Welsh says, are four:

1. Lacking a good "Hook Tweet".
2. No "headers" on the "body" Tweets.
3. Way too wordy, and no white space for reading.
4. No clear call-to-action or call-to-conversation at the end.

Read Justin Welsh's insightful blog, "The System Behind 9 Twitter Threads With 6M+ Impressions" justinwelsh.me/blog/03192022

So, remember your hook—it's *key*. And remember that you'll need to 'train' ChatGPT and other AI writing tools, by repetitions with the tool and better input, to give you the best output.

Here's what ChatGPT gave me when I asked it to help me start a Twitter thread on content marketing:

write a twitter thread on content marketing

 1/ Content marketing is the process of creating, publishing and distributing content that aims to attract, engage and retain a target audience. It's about telling a story and building a relationship with your audience.

2/ The key to successful content marketing is understanding your target audience and creating content that resonates with them. This could include blog posts, videos, infographics, podcasts, and more.

3/ Consistency is crucial in content marketing. Regularly publishing high-quality content helps establish your brand as a thought leader in your industry and keeps your audience engaged.

4/ Content marketing can also be used to achieve specific business goals, such as increasing website traffic, generating leads, and boosting conversions. It's important to set clear and measurable goals for your content marketing efforts.

5/ Don't be afraid to experiment with different types of content to see what resonates with your audience. This could include trying new formats, such as live videos or interactive quizzes.

Eh. Not bad, but not great, right? Let's work with ChatGPT to make it better.

First, I asked it to give me a more compelling hook:

give me a compelling hook for this twitter thread

"Unlock the Power of Storytelling with Content Marketing: A Comprehensive Guide to Boost Your Brand and Grow Your Business."

I took that hook, and rewrote it, and then—*get this! ready for it?*—I *asked* ChatGPT if it would like to see how I rewrote the piece. Why? Because I'm *training* it on my style. ChatGPT responded like a very nice, positive human being would. (These robots are crazy!)

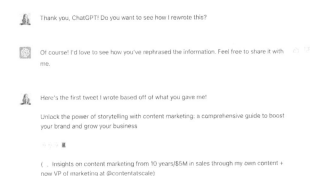

Thank you, ChatGPT! Do you want to see how I rewrote this?

Of course! I'd love to see how you've rephrased the information. Feel free to share it with me.

Here's the first tweet I wrote based off of what you gave me!

Unlock the power of storytelling with content marketing: a comprehensive guide to boost your brand and grow your business

(Insights on content marketing from 10 years/$5M in sales through my own content + now VP of marketing at @contentatscale)

Now, look at *this*. Based on the content I wrote, the idea for which didn't have to come from the dreaded blank slate—but instead, it came directly from AI! Remember our writer's hat:

The writer's hat material

Read Every Day
Use AI to dramatically reduce blank-page syndrome
Invest in Yourself

I was able to write something *better,* and then feed it back *into* AI, which is now writing content *even better than me* based on what I gave it. See this in action— and specifically look at that last sentence by ChatGPT: "from 10+ years in the game…to now leading the marketing charge"—that's *great* copy!

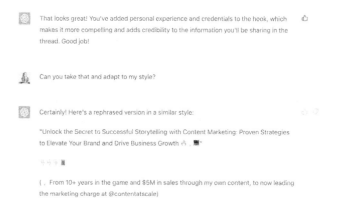

That looks great! You've added personal experience and credentials to the hook, which makes it more compelling and adds credibility to the information you'll be sharing in the thread. Good job!

Can you take that and adapt to my style?

Certainly! Here's a rephrased version in a similar style:

"Unlock the Secret to Successful Storytelling with Content Marketing: Proven Strategies to Elevate Your Brand and Drive Business Growth 🔥 📷"

(, From 10+ years in the game and $5M in sales through my own content, to now leading the marketing charge at @contentatscale)

Unbelievable. We're living in new times!

My CTA for this Twitter thread was very simple: subscribe to the newsletter.

Julia McCoy @JuliaEMcCoy · 13m   ...
For more insights like this, subscribe to my weekly newsletter:

contenthacker.com
The Content Hacker™ List | Subscribe Today
Hear directly from Julia. Subscribe today to get a FREE copy of our
Starter Kit and Julia's handwritten notes in your email!

    ○   ⇄   ♡   �.ıl 10   ↑

The C.L.E.A.R. Formula for Social Media Posts

Muddled writing is the number one killer of social media posts.

And when I say "muddled", I mean murky. Unclear. Full of fluff that gets in the way of your story, your meaning, your point.

Because you need readers to "get it" immediately with a social post. They're about two seconds away from scrolling past your efforts at any time, so you need to ensure they're with you and nodding their heads at every word.

Using a formula, therefore, is an intelligent way to ensure your words are honed and your meaning gets through. Because just telling a rambling story and posting it is like aiming for a bullseye in the pitch dark. There's no way of knowing if your shot will land. Don't do this—turn on some lights and perfect your strategy, trajectory, and aim! You need to ensure your story has an impact (that it entertains, educates, or empowers someone) AND that it's crafted to get read.

That's what the C.L.E.A.R. formula helps you do: Cut the fluff, cut to the point, and **entertain**, **educate**, or **empower** someone with your message and story. Think of it as a strategy for writing social media posts. It's a vehicle you can set your story inside, complete with an engine to take your message as far as it will go.

This framework is the brainchild of **Jeff Hunter**,[19] a savvy marketer who runs his own businesses—**Savage**

---

[19] Savage Marketer: https://jeffjhunter.com; VA Staffer: https://vastaffer.com

Marketer and **VA Staffer**—and knows how to communicate online to get results. I can attest to those results, by the way. Every time I've used this formula to write a social media post and share a story, it's gotten traction, as you'll soon see.

Story, by the way, rests at the heart of the C.L.E.A.R. formula. That's important to understand—your social media writing prowess rests on clear and concise **storytelling** more than anything. And it's not just any old storytelling; it's a method of writing that helps you give value to your reader within the **framework** of an engaging story. That, my friends, leads to results.

So, what is the C.L.E.A.R. formula? It looks like this:

1. **C**uriosity
2. **L**ead-in Pitch
3. **E**motion
4. **A**nalyze/Proof
5. **R**einforce/Reaction/Result

Before we get into how to write each piece of the formula, we first must make sure you have good stories to use to fit inside the framework.

How to Find Stories to Fit Inside the C.L.E.A.R. Formula

Before you can tell a good story, you first need a compelling topic. For example, if I tell a story about what I had for breakfast this morning, that's not necessarily interesting. If I tell a story about how what I had for breakfast changed the course of my entire day/week/month, I'm onto something.

What's the difference between the two topics above? **Vulnerability**.

The first topic doesn't necessarily cost me anything to tell. It reveals nothing deeper about me. The second topic, however, is the exact opposite. To tell you that story, I need to get real. I need to reveal aspects of myself that might have been hidden or unknown previously. To tell that story truthfully and well, I need to effectively hand you a piece of myself on a platter. And that's hard to do.

But it's more worthy. By sharing myself vulnerably, I will draw my audience closer to me (or to my brand). I'll seem more human, more relatable, more real. That will build a relationship with my audience, because it will help them know me (or the brand) more intimately. And that's the goal.

With all that in mind, here are my suggestions for story sources to mine for gold and use inside your C.L.E.A.R. formula:

1. **Interactions with ideal clients** – What questions have they asked you? What struggles do you/did you help them overcome?
2. **You (or the brand's) vulnerable truths** – Personal business demons and how you overcame them
3. **The sacred cows you kill in your industry** – The myths you dispel or prove wrong

Tips for Telling Viral-Worthy Stories on Social Media

1. **Be vulnerable. No, *really* vulnerable.** Go deep and share a story that matters to you. If it doesn't matter, it's not worth telling.

2. **Know who you're writing to.** You need to understand your target audience, including what they'll relate to, what language will hit home with them, and the problems they face. Do NOT guess.

3. **Zero in on your hook.** Your hook is everything. If it's not good enough, people will scroll right past your post. The curiosity you pique with those first words often determines the level of success overall. As such, take your time with the hook. Play with wording and sentence structure as well as the main idea or thought you share in those crucial lines. (Even swapping out one single verb or adjective might make a giant difference.) Write multiple versions until you arrive at the strongest hook possible.

   i. *For a primer on writing good hooks, return to Chapter 1: Email Writing.*

4. **Stick to the framework.** This is a winning formula for a reason: It works. Every post I have written with this structure has done well, and some of them were viral hits that received hundreds of thousands of views.

5. **Get other eyes on it.** Sending your C.L.E.A.R. story to a trusted friend or peer is a good way to test it out. There's a lot your eyes can miss, so don't be afraid to ask for feedback or edits on your post draft.

Write Your C.L.E.A.R. Story

Once you have a good story in hand, it's time to fit it inside the C.L.E.A.R. framework. Let's break it down, step by step, using a real-life story I shared on social media that went viral.

The story I used: I shared a vulnerable story about the struggle of hiring a good writer.

Results: 50k views on LinkedIn, 100+ engagements on Facebook, 200+ engagements on Instagram

1. Curiosity

This is the first line of your post—your hook, your headline, your attention-grabber. It should incite curiosity in your readers, grabbing them and not letting go. You need to stop people in their scroll with your hook.

Be brief with this. Try to keep it to a few words, or one sentence tops. Play with wording, especially phrasing, to cut as much fluff as possible.

Fluffy example: "There was no doubt about it. It sucked."

This can be cut down to:

"It sucked." **(The hook I actually used.)**

Why can't we go with the first example? The first sentence adds nothing to the meaning of our hook. It's a filler phrase. We can whittle it down to "It sucked" and the hook is instantly punchier, clearer, and far more emphatic. Moral of the story: Don't be afraid to ruthlessly cut down your paragraphs and sentences until they're minimal but full of power.

Furthermore, this hook works because I'm sharing a relatable feeling, one my target audience (in this case, executives) understands. It also makes them ask—WHAT sucked?? Curiosity, people!

2. Lead-in Pitch

Think of your lead-in pitch as the fishing line attached to your hook.

The hook is what grabs them, but the lead-in pitch is what pulls them in. After reading this part, the reader should want to know more and read more.

As a general rule, keep your lead-in pitch to a few sentences (1-2 is ideal). These should continue to **emphasize and/or explain** the idea, mood, feeling, or statement you made in your hook, drawing out that curiosity into interest.

Let me show you how I did that in my real social media post.

Hook: "It sucked."

From here, I answer the questions "WHAT sucked and WHY?" I create a scene that establishes what my post is about while drawing in readers.

Lead-in pitch: *"I put a month, countless hours, and a few late nights into training a new agency writer this April. And today, I had to reassign their work.*

"They hadn't bothered to read or implement my latest feedback, and completely ignored it. Deadlines were missed, work backlogged."

In a few sentences, I tell you the problem I faced and how I struggled. I piggy-back off of my hook. I write in a relatable way to my target audience, who have probably dealt with the same issue.

Let your lead-in pitch set the scene as you draw them in.

3. Emotion

Next: Find the emotion in the story you're telling. Reflect on your hook and your lead-in pitch, and ask yourself, "How did it make me feel? How did it affect me?"

Again, keep this super brief. One line or even one word can do some heavy lifting here. With that in mind, choose your verbs and adjectives carefully. Go for the power-punchers. Nix any weak words that don't carry the weight of the emotion you're sharing.

Example: *"I saw massive talent in their work early on. But, I'd been blindsided."*

What are my power-punchers in this sentence? "Massive" (the talent of the writer I was training was HUGE) and "blindsided" (I was so excited about having them on my team, I was literally BLIND to how they weren't a good fit).

Imagine, for a minute, that I had chosen weaker words to use in this line.

Weak example: "I saw a lot of talent in their work early on. But, I was wrong."

Do you see the difference in the strength and impact of the emotion I'm sharing, just by swapping two words? Similarly, look for weak words in your writing to root out (any word that's cliché, wimpy, or lifeless) and replace them with power-punchers (words that punch your reader in the gut with their impact).

Also, avoid any weak word paired with a modifier like "really" or "very." Replace with a strong adjective that does all the descriptive work in one word. (This is especially important for the emotion portion of the C.L.E.A.R. formula, but it's also a good practice for all of your descriptive writing.)

Examples of Weak Words	Replace with:
Happy	Joyful, content, elated, blissful
Nice	Delightful, charming, heartwarming, captivating
Good, amazing	Astonishing, mind-boggling, awe-inspiring, enthralling
Sad	Depressed, sorrowful, mournful, miserable, despondent
Wrong	Bogus, flawed, askew, misguided
Tired	Exhausted, depleted, weary, drained
Examples of Weak Words + Modifiers	Replace with:
Very pretty	Beautiful, gorgeous, stunning
Really bad	Terrible, horrible, dreadful, atrocious
Very hard	Impossible, grueling, demanding, brutal
Super angry	Furious, enraged, livid, incensed
Incredibly big	Huge, humongous, monstrous, giant, enormous

4. Analyze/Proof

Here's the meat of your C.L.E.A.R. post. This is where you write out the analysis/proof of your content in 2-6 sentences.

Analyze the problem you talked about in the previous three sections: hook, lead-in pitch, and emotion. What did you find out from experiencing what you experienced? What, ultimately, was the learning moment?

Example: *"You can have talent…*

But if your attitude is wrong…

If you aren't willing to try harder, get back up, and embrace change…

Your talent ends up in a discarded heap.

In Gary Halpert's Boron Letters (Gary has had more multi-million dollar winning campaigns than any other copywriter ever), he said enthusiasm wins over talent, every time.

In Grit, celebrated researcher and professor Dr. Angela Duckworth proves that achievement doesn't come from talent… it comes from perseverance."

As you can see, in this section, I tell you what I learned from my experience hiring a writer with massive talent, only to end up reassigning their work. I expand on the main kernel of learning I discovered (talent means nothing if you have the wrong attitude) by mentioning outside sources that underlined this truth for me (in my case, it was two books by experts). I'm offering further **proof** beyond my experience that this truth is universal.

This section is a good place to get a little philosophical, to lean into hard truths and the surprising discoveries you've made as a result. Your proof might include wisdom from books you've read, hard-hitting statistics from relevant studies, the words of a known expert, or even similar experiences you've had in the past that never sunk in until they were repeated.

Though you want to give yourself space for analysis in this section, remember to economize with your words. Write out the meat of what you want to say, then ruthlessly cut it down until only the most important pieces remain.

5. Reinforce/Reaction/Result

After your analysis, it's time to share the **result** of what you learned and how you **reacted** in 1-3 sentences. At the same time, you'll be **reinforcing** your original lead-in pitch.

This is the place to drive home the major takeaways from your other C.L.E.A.R. sections. It's also somewhat future-oriented: How will what you learned from this experience change your approach moving forward? How has it changed you *forever*?

Example: *"I've read the books I quoted.*

But I keep learning the hard way.

Take it from me. Perseverance, grit, and the right attitude ALWAYS outperform talent.

I've trained and mentored writers at the top of their craft... but when I look back, they didn't show talent. They showed up with a great attitude.

That thing you're stuck doing? It's okay to not have the answers today. What's NOT okay is giving up. Keep going. You'll win."

See how I focus on my major takeaway from this whole experience (that the right attitude outperforms talent)? I take it one further, though: I apply this way of thinking to any obstacle you, my reader, might face. I turn it back to my audience in the final sentences, which is great for maintaining engagement. In the end, it's not just about me, but how I can share what I've learned to help others.

Put It All Together

With each section of your C.L.E.A.R. post written, you can put them all together.

At this point, I would continue tweaking the post as a whole for flow, succinctness, and impact. Identify any fluffy wording and hone it down so it's sharper and clearer. Replace weak words with stronger ones. Rewrite any sentences or ideas that are muddled.

Once all this is done, celebrate! You've just written your first C.L.E.A.R. social media post.

So you can see a complete post in action, here are all the pieces of my C.L.E.A.R. story reassembled:

Example:

Checklist for Social Media Writing

- AVOID the number one killer of social media posts dependent on text (think: long captions, text-only posts on Facebook or LinkedIn): **muddled, bloated writing**.

- AVOID the number two killer: **unclear, rambling storytelling** with no purpose or strategy behind it.

- Vet the stories you want to share on social before you blindly post: Will they **entertain**, **educate**, or **empower** your audience? Will your audience CARE?

o Use a proven formula like C.L.E.A.R. to structure the stories you share on social for more impact and better engagement.

o Edit, edit, edit! Get rid of fluffy sentences, weak words, and general bloat in your social media writing. **If you can say it in one word or one sentence, don't use a paragraph**.

o Spend time crafting your social media writing with care. For example, don't dash off a hook in two minutes. Write the first draft, and then hone it, edit it, tweak it, and play with it until it's the best version of itself.

o Remember: Social media posts may take you MORE time to craft because of how vital each word is in a short post. Give yourself plenty of time to do so.

Social Media Writing Outline: The C.L.E.A.R. Formula

*Credits go to **Jeff Hunter**, original creator of C.L.E.A.R. (**jeffjhunter.com**)*

1. **C**URIOSITY – Write your curiosity headline (should only be a few words or one sentence tops)
2. **L**EAD-IN PITCH – Write down a couple of sentences that draw them in. They want to read more, know more, after reading this. (Should be 1-2 sentences tops)
3. **E**MOTION – How did it make you feel? How did it affect you? (One sentence or even one word)
4. **A**NALYZE/PROOF – This is the MEAT of your post. Write down your analysis/proof of your content here. What did you find out, and learn from? (2-6 sentences)
5. **R**EINFORCE/REACTION/RESULT – What was it you learned? This should reinforce the original lead-in pitch. Get them engaged. Write down your reinforcement/reaction/result here. (1-3 sentences)

CHAPTER 4:

SEO Blog Writing

Going into this chapter, there's something you need to know.

Most blog content sucks.

That isn't hyperbole, either; it's the truth. 90.63% of web pages get zero traffic from Google.[20] (That means they don't rank on page one because they suck.) 95% of all pages get zero backlinks.[21] (That means most blogs aren't worth mentioning or citing because they suck.)

Most blog content sucks, but that doesn't mean YOUR content will suck.

Follow me through this chapter, and it won't. *Promise.*

---

[20] Tim Soulo. (2020, Jan. 31). "90.63% of Content Gets No Traffic From Google. And How to Be in the Other 9.37% [New Research for 2020]." Ahrefs blog. https://ahrefs.com/blog/search-traffic-study/
[21] Brian Dean. (2020, April 28). "We Analyzed 11.8 Million Google Search Results: Here's What We Learned About SEO." Backlinko. https://backlinko.com/search-engine-ranking

The only drawback: To achieve non-suckiness, you will have to put in some effort and investment. But it will be worth it.

Why?

Because, when done right, SEO blog content is **humble-but-mighty**.

Humble, because blog posts are worth a penny per dozen on the internet. They're everywhere, on every topic. Nearly 2 billion websites exist online, and nearly 600 million have blogs.[22] BUT—a humble blog post can nurture your audience better than any advertisement, or any social media post. AND—since there are millions of sucky blogs out there, yours will stand out as a shining golden ray of light if you back it with some solid techniques.

Mighty, because even just **one** well-written and optimized post on your website can be enough to convince someone of your credibility, expertise, and authority—and make them want to buy. This has happened to me numerous times. We put out high-quality, well-written, keyword-optimized blog posts. An ideal client searches for their problem on Google, finds one of our blogs, reads it… and then converts—that day!

So, as you can see, the humble-but-mighty SEO blog can be the crème de la crème of your SEO content marketing strategy. These blogs will work behind the scenes to pull in ideal traffic. They'll nurture would-be

---

[22] First Site Guide. (2022, Sept. 28). "Blogging Statistics 2022: Ultimate List with 47 Facts and Stats." https://firstsiteguide.com/blogging-stats/

perfect customers… so those "would-bes" become *actual* perfect customers. And all you have to do is write them.

It's not difficult. You just need a process and toolbox for writing amazing SEO blog content. And, once you know and understand this process inside-out, you can even implement AI writing tools to help you speed up the process while still putting out great blogs stamped with your brand's unique fingerprints.

Allow me to share it all with you from A to Z. But first…

Note One: Since the scope of this book is about *writing* content, that's what we'll stick to in this chapter—how to *write* SEO blog content. We're assuming you already have done your topic and keyword research and have them firmly in hand. If you haven't done either, yet—STOP. Do not pass "Go." You need **a solid topic mapped to a keyword** to continue.

Note Two: We will cover how to *dramatically* speed up your time and process with AI writing now as the baseline (think: literally a robot hand can now write the majority of your blog content, and, it's good). But first, you should understand what goes into a good SEO blog post, so your knowledge stands firm—with or without the robots.

Need to learn how to generate content topics and research keywords? These are pieces of content strategy I teach in my courses and mentorship. Learn more in contenthacker.com.

5 Key Pieces of an SEO Blog Post

How do you construct a solid SEO blog post? Let's start by breaking down the key pieces that every SEO blog post needs to be strong and effective.

1. **Headline and introduction (the hook)** – The headline is your title, or H1 (more on headers below). The hook is the one-two punch of your headline + your introductory paragraph. Together, these two elements serve to catch the reader's interest immediately and pull them further into your post.

2. **Main points** (headers, or H2s) and **supporting points** (subheaders, or H3s) – Each blog should contain at least one main point you're trying to make about the topic, plus any points that support those main points.

3. **Content & supporting visuals** – Break down and explain your points using your expertise, research, statistics, and visuals.

4. **Calls-to-action, or CTAs** – Each blog needs at least one CTA to cash in on the trust you've built with the reader. Call them to the next action they can take after they're done reading.

5. **Conclusion** (final main point, or H2) – Finish with a conclusion that wraps up the post and offers at least one takeaway for the reader. In the final paragraphs of the conclusion, end in a soft sell to your most relevant landing page or sales page.

We Need to Talk About Headers

At every point in this chapter, you'll see me talk about headers (also called *headings*). These are vital pieces for both readers and search engines, so they deserve some explanation and thought. (If you're familiar with headers and use them correctly already, feel free to skip this section.)

Headers, as you'll recall, are the titles and headings inside a blog post that organize the information and break it up into sections. For online content displayed on a web page or blog, headers are denoted with HTML code, like this:

```
<h1>Title of Page</h1>

Introduction.

<h2>First Main Point</h2>

<h3>Supporting point</h3>
```

Here's how that looks on a blog:

Content Hacker™   ABOUT   BLOG   PODCAST   WORK WITH US   FREE TRAINING

H1 The Psychology of Colors: How to Choose Personal Branding Colors That Pop

by Julia McCoy November 19, 2022

Colors are incredible.

They have the power to influence our mood, to attract or repel us, and to draw up distinctive memories and associations.

That's why businesses use personal branding colors in strategic ways. They know specific colors will **project the right image and draw the right audience**.

For instance:

- The color pink can make us think of soft stuffed animals, cotton candy, and babies. 🧸
- The color blue might soothe our minds, remind us of the sky or the ocean, or even make us feel depressed. 🌊
- We might be drawn to the color green, repelled by red, or have happy memories associated with yellow. 😊

85.3% of consumers say **color is the primary reason they buy a product...**

And 80% say **color helps increase brand recognition**.

So you can see why choosing the right personal branding colors is essential.

Your branding is your calling card online. It appears everywhere – on your website, on social media, in your email signature, on your content, and beyond.

Using the right personal branding colors could mean the difference between attracting your ideal customers or turning them away.

The colors you choose should represent your brand identity, what you value, and what you hope to achieve.

In other words, how do you want the world to see your business? Your branding colors can help make it happen.

H2 ## How to Choose Personal Branding Colors & Project the Right Image

I discuss this topic on my podcast, too. 🎙 Listen to the episode to learn about the psychology of colors and how to choose your best branding colors.

H3 ### 1. Know the Psychology of Colors and What They Communicate

Color psychology is a great place to start when choosing your personal branding colors. This is the study of how each color affects our moods, perceptions, and emotions.

Colors are powerful communicators. Thus, the question color psychology seeks to answer is, **"What messages does each color communicate?"** These may stem from cultural traditions, nature, symbolism, pop culture, folklore, trends, and more.

And, in a word processor like Microsoft Word, headings are formatting you can apply to pieces of text, like this:

Title of Page (Heading 1, or H1)

Note how, both in HTML code *and* in text editors/word processing software, headers/headings have assigned numerical levels (i.e., Heading 1, Heading 2, H1, H2, etc.). There's a good reason for that! The numerical level of a heading tells us what role it plays on the page and its importance overall.

- **H1, or Heading 1**: Page title.
- **H2, or Heading 2**: Main points.
- **H3, or Heading 3:** Subpoints that support a main point/H2. H3s can *only* appear underneath an H2 and support that H2—they never stand alone or appear under the H1. They're always nested inside a related H2.
- **H4, or Heading 4**: Sub-subpoints that support a subpoint/H3. H4s can *only* appear underneath a related H3. They never stand alone.
- **H5, or Heading 5**: Sub-sub-subpoints that support an H4. (You'll rarely to never use H5s in a blog post, so don't worry about them.)
- **H6, or Heading 6**: Sub-sub-sub-subpoints (phew!) that support an H5. (Ditto with H6s—you'll never use these.)

So, why do we care so much about these silly little headers?

First, remember that headers help you create the overarching **structure** of your page. Much like the framework of a house, the structure of your blog helps hold everything together so it makes sense. You can see this in action if you delete the body content from a blog and just leave the headers behind, like this:

The Psychology of Colors: How to Choose Personal Branding Colors That Pop

How to Choose Personal Branding Colors & Project the Right Image

1. Know the Psychology of Colors and What They Communicate

2. Connect Brand Adjectives to Colors

3. Choose a Brand Color Palette

4. Consider Color Theory

5. Don't Choose Personal Branding Colors Based on Your Preferences Alone

Personal Branding Colors: Build Your Brand One Brick at a Time

Read this post in full: ***contenthacker.com/personal-branding-colors***

For readers, header formatting on a web page helps us immediately understand the relationships between sections at a glance. The H1 is the largest and most important because it's the page title. H2s are second-largest because these are the main points breaking down the topic, H3s are third-largest, and so on.

Headers also help us scan the page and quickly find the information that interests us most, or answers our questions. (79% of people scan web pages instead of reading them; only 16% always read word-by-word![23]) Without headers, we wouldn't know where to find the information about color theory in the blog above, for example. We would have to hunt through paragraphs of text that all ran together in a giant word wall. It would be a much more frustrating experience.

For search engines, headers denoted in HTML code help algorithms understand what the page is about, which information is most important, and how sections relate to each other. And when a search engine algorithm has a better understanding of your page topic and how you address it, it has a better understanding of how to rank your page in its results for a specific keyword.

Here's an easy way to think about headers: Imagine your blog post is a book with each main header (H2) representing a book chapter, and each subheader (H3) representing a section of a chapter. You can use sub-subheaders (H4s) as needed to further break down sections. For example:

- Title (H1)
    - Chapter One (H2)
        - Section A (H3)

---

[23] Jakob Nielsen. (1997, Sept. 30) "How Users Read on the Web." Nielsen Norman Group. https://www.nngroup.com/articles/how-users-read-on-the-web/

- Section A.1 (H4)
- Section A.2 (H4)
  - Section B (H3)
  - Section C (H3)
- Chapter Two (H2)
  - Section A (H3)
  - Section B (H3)
- Chapter Three (H2)
  - Section A (H3)
  - Section B (H3)
    - Section B.1 (H4)
    - Section B.2 (H4)
  - Section C (H3)
  - Section D (H3)
- Conclusion (H2)

Lastly, the headers inside the SEO blogs you create should be optimized with keywords, including your focus keyword, related keywords, and synonyms. Here's a good overview of how to do that:

- **H1/page title**: Include your focus keyword in your title, near the beginning.
- **H2**: Include your focus keyword in at least one H2 on the page. Include a related keyword or synonym in at least one additional H2 (depending on your page structure and how many H2s you have).
- **H3**: Include your focus keyword in at least one H3. Include a related keyword or synonym in at least one additional H3

(again, depending on your page's particular structure.

See how that works?

To sum up, headers *aren't* random or meaningless. They're not just a quick way to format your text—in fact, you shouldn't be using them to format text at all. Instead, headers give helpful clues and cues to readers and search engines about the information on your page. They improve readability, organize your content, and help search engines understand the topic of your page better. Never leave home without headers in your SEO blogs—they're vital.

More Best Practices for Formatting SEO Blogs

Headers are one of the biggies for formatting SEO blogs correctly. But what else do you need to consider?

1. **Outline your post beforehand**. Jot down your blog topic/title, then list the main points you want to make in the post. Refine these points and rearrange until the order and flow make sense. Then apply headings in whichever text editor you're using (WordPress, Word, etc.) so your page structure is set.

2. **Shorten your paragraphs**. In a book, long paragraphs make sense because books are usually read on a printed page. In a blog, shorter paragraphs make sense because most people read them on computer screens or the tiny electronic rectangle of their smartphone screens. Shorter paragraphs are easier on the eyes—and the attention span. Rule of

thumb: Three sentences per paragraph or fewer. (I'm personally a fan of the one-sentence paragraph, especially in introductions.)

3. **Shorten your sentences**. Break up run-on sentences into smaller pieces. Untangle complex sentences and simplify them.

4. **Write in the second-person perspective**. Address the reader directly, as if they're sitting across from you at a table and you're having a conversation.

5. **Include relevant images and visuals**. Visuals break up the text and provide your eyes with relief. Visuals are also engaging, especially when they further illustrate a concept or idea you're discussing in the text. (More on using visuals in SEO blogs later in this chapter.)

Keyword Usage for SEO Blog Posts: An Overview

A lot of newbie content writers find search engine optimization and keyword usage intimidating. "How many times are you supposed to insert the main keyword again? Where does it go? How do you use keywords naturally?"

The truth is, you're probably overcomplicating it. Instead, remember these three things, and you'll master keyword usage for SEO writing.

1. **Insert the keyword in strategic places**. Keep a checklist of these places handy so you don't forget any. After a while, this will become second nature and you won't need the list.

(You'll find my recommended keyword usage checklist below.)

2. **Write about the topic to help the reader**. The keyword (and its variations) will naturally fall into place if you approach each SEO blog from the perspective of *what the reader doesn't know*. Put yourself in their shoes. How do you bridge the gap between their problem—or their lack of knowledge—and the solution? A naturally keyword-rich blog will be the byproduct of describing, explaining, and teaching the topic so the reader reaches this understanding.

3. **Sounding natural trumps awkward keyword usage**. Never use a keyword if/when it sounds unnatural or forced. Forget counting keywords, as well. The number of times you include it doesn't matter. Instead, it's about whether or not your writing is topically-relevant, helpful to the reader, and satisfying to read.

Keyword Usage Checklist

Insert the **primary/focus keyword** in these places, using the exact-match phrase (as long as it makes sense—if it won't, slight variations are fine):

- ○ **H1/page title** – once
- ○ **SEO title/meta title** – once, near the beginning of the title
- ○ **Meta description** – once, near the beginning of the description

- o **Introduction** – once, preferably in the first paragraph
- o **H2s** – at least once, more for longer blogs with multiple H2s
- o **H3s** – at least once, more for longer blogs with multiple H3s
- o **Body text** – n/a, include naturally (which means don't think about it at all; just try to be helpful and explain the topic)
- o **Image alt text**[24] – use once per alt text description (but only for topic-relevant images in your blog)

Insert any **secondary keywords, variations/synonymous terms, or related terms** in these places:
- o **Introduction** – naturally
- o **H2s** – once or twice, but only if there are multiple H2s on the page
- o **H3s** – once or twice, but only if there are multiple H3s on the page
- o **Body text** – naturally throughout
- o **Image alt text** – when describing relevant images
- o **Internal links** – when linking to related content on your website

---

[24] Image alt text helps search engines understand what an image is about. Most content management systems like WordPress have options for adding image alt text to each uploaded image. Learn more: *https://blog.hubspot.com/marketing/image-alt-text*

>>**When in doubt**: Skip using the keyword to avoid overuse and keyword stuffing.

I teach all of this and more inside my writing courses. If you need extra help with these concepts, including 1:1 guidance, consider enrolling today:
contenthacker.com/writingcourses

How to Write an SEO Blog Post

Ready to write? Let's construct an SEO blog post from the top down, from headline to conclusion. I'll reference an actual post from the Content Hacker blog that's ranking #1 for its keyword to show you the concepts in action. Here's the post we're referencing: *contenthacker.com/content-marketing-worth*

Let's do this.

Blog Prep: Outlining

Before you write a single word of your introduction or craft a headline, I urge you to first *write an outline of the entire blog post*.

Outlining is immensely helpful for a few reasons: 1.) It helps you lay out your post and hone what you'll talk about. This keeps you from rambling or going on unnecessary tangents. 2.) It structures your post, dividing it into logical sections so it's easier to scan and read. 3.) It gives you natural places to add headings and keywords. 4.) It makes the actual writing easier because you can just fill in each section. 5.) It's easier to organize your points when you outline them, first. Then you can rearrange and play with the order without messing with paragraphs of text.

Luckily, outlining can be incredibly simple. Just open up a blank document. Type in your working title, blog topic, or focus keyword. Underneath that, jot down your main points in a list. Do you plan on breaking down any of your main points further? Write down those subpoints, too. Then apply a heading structure to the page (H1 for the title, H2 for main points, H3 for subpoints). Here's what a rough, working outline for our example blog would look like. In this version, we still need to finalize our headline/H1, but the main points and subpoints are all set.

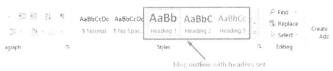

Blog outline with headers set

Keyword/blog topic: Why is content marketing worth 400 billion H1

Introduction

Content Marketing Isn't New H2

1. User Demands Make Most Online Advertising Obsolete H3

2. Customers Expect Useful Content H3

3. Google Expects Useful Content H3

Why Is Content Marketing So Profitable? H2

1. It's Got a Crazy High ROI H3

2. It's Future-Proof H3

3. It's Cheaper than Other Digital Marketing Tactics H3

4. There's No Talking Without Walking H3

Grow Authority, Not Advertising Spend H2

Conclusion

With your outline complete, it's time to dive deep into writing. Here's a refresher on the pieces we'll be crafting:

1. Headline and introduction (the hook)
2. Main points and subpoints (headers and subheaders)
3. Content & visuals
4. Calls-to-action (CTAs)
5. Conclusion

1. Headline and Introduction (the Hook)

By now, if you're reading this handbook in order and have already gone through *Chapter 1: Email Writing*, you're a bit more comfortable with writing both headlines and hooks, right?

That said, writing these pieces for blogs is necessarily different. We'll start with SEO blog headlines.

❖ *Headlines and SEO*

The headline isn't just the title of your blog post. It's also the first thing a searcher will read in search results. It will help them determine whether your article will give them the information they need, or whether it will be interesting to read.

Before we get into actually writing headlines, we need to first address the SEO elephant in the room. Headlines are monumentally important for SEO because they contain some of the most important information on the page.

As such, on your blog, your headline graces the top, like a king lording over his subjects. In HTML code, it will be denoted with the only H1 tag that will appear in the entire stretch of code for that page. (The H1 tag simply tells the browser AND search engines that whatever text appears inside the tag is the most important heading on the page. And, of course, the most important page heading is always the **title**.)

```
<header class="entry-header">
<div class="entry-meta">
<span class="category-meta"><a href="https://contenthacker.com/content-marketing/">Content Marketing</a></span> </div>
<h1 class="entry-title">Why Content Marketing Is Worth $400 Billion-And Is About to Skyrocket to $600 Billion</h1>
<div class="entry-meta">
<div class="author-avatar">
```

What considerations do we need to make for a good SEO headline?

Page title vs. SEO title. With your headline, you need to be thinking about both the page title (the H1) *and* the SEO title. What's the difference? The **page title** will appear on your blog page at the top of the content. The **SEO title** (also called the meta title) will appear in search engine results.

Why Content Marketing Is Worth $400 Billion— And Is About to Skyrocket to $600 Billion

by Julia McCoy October 6, 2021

Page title/headline
(appears at top of blog post)

We've known for a few years now that content marketing would be worth just over $400 billion in 2021. There was no stopping the revolution underway.

And if the research is to be believed, it's going to grow another $200 billion or so by 2024, bringing the total worth to over **$600 billion in 2024.**

And guess what the TOP outsourced activity is?

...Content creation.

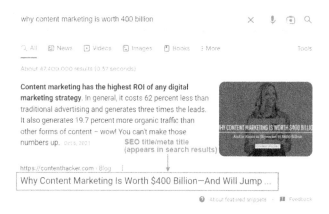

Now, you can use the same headline for both instances, or you can use different versions of the same headline. The latter option makes the most sense when you come up with a great headline, but it won't fit the character requirements for appearing in search results (up to 60 characters long). In that instance, you could use the original headline for your page title, and tweak it slightly for your SEO title so it displays fully in search results without getting cut off.

In a WordPress setup with the Yoast SEO plugin,[25] the page title and the SEO title are entered in different input boxes, making it easy for you to differentiate and set both. The page title input box appears at the top of the "Edit Post"/"Add Post" page:

---

[25] A great plugin for helping you nail SEO in your blogs, while offering an easy way to add meta titles and descriptions to each post *without* having to dink around with html code. *https://yoast.com*

And the SEO title input box appears at the bottom, with the other Yoast SEO settings:

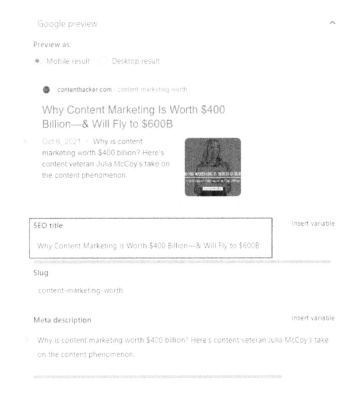

Character limit. As I mentioned, search engine results will only display up to 60 characters of any given title/headline. That's a consideration for SEO because, usually, you want your full title to be displayed without getting cut off. If your headline is snipped, it might eliminate an important piece of information you want your audience to know. For that reason, try to condense your SEO titles to fit in the character limit.

Keyword usage. Finally, keyword usage matters greatly to create a good SEO headline. Include the keyword you want to rank for in your title, try to use the exact-match term (for instance, "SEO marketing" vs. a variation like "marketing and SEO"), and add it close to the beginning of the phrase. (Example: "SEO Marketing: A Beginner's Guide" would be preferable to "A Beginner's Guide to SEO Marketing" because the keyword, "SEO marketing", appears at the beginning of the title.)

Now that you're thinking about both what search engines want AND what readers need, let's get into writing effective headlines that get clicks in search engine results and make people want to read your posts.

❖ *How to Write an SEO Headline*

First, start with your focus keyword. You MUST include it in your headline if you want to rank for that term. Including it will also help you stay topic-focused so you can truly define for readers what your blog post is about.

Next, tell readers what to expect. What, exactly, does your blog post cover? What information will they find inside? Be more specific than you'd think.

Poor example: "All About Content Marketing" (This is incredibly vague—what *about* content marketing?)

Better example: "10 Key Content Marketing Concepts" (An improvement—this is more specific partly because of the inclusion of the number 10, which tells the reader exactly how much information to expect.)

After that, add some value. How can you position your headline in terms of benefits for your audience? How will reading your post help them?

Even better example: "10 Key Content Marketing Concepts You Must Know to Be Successful" (Reading the post will help them be more knowledgeable *and* successful with content marketing. Huge benefits!)

At this point, you might be thinking, "Cool, I guess we're done writing the headline, right?"

Nope. Not even close.

There are still ways to make it better.

Go even further by pumping up the language in your headline. Look for areas where you could insert stronger verbs, adjectives, and adverbs. Play around with word usage and phrasing. Whip out your dusty old thesaurus from college (or open a new browser tab with your favorite online version) and go spelunking for some snappy verbiage.

We're-getting-close-to-great example: "10 Killer Content Marketing Concepts You Must Know (or You'll Fail)" (Do you see where I replaced specific words and phrases to punch up the language? "Key" was nixed in favor of "Killer." I tossed out "to Be Successful" and went for the opposite outcome: "or You'll Fail"—and suddenly, this headline just got a lot peppier.)

We could stop here.

But to achieve greatness, we need to go further. We need to push this to the limit. I call this part "throwing everything you've got at the wall and seeing what sticks."

Here are the additional versions I wrote at this stage. All I did was play with wording, keeping the main structure I established in my second draft intact.

- "10 Cornerstone Concepts of Content Marketing to Clinch That ROI"
- "10 Bedrock Content Marketing Concepts All Marketers Should Know"
- "10 Key Content Marketing Concepts You Must Know for Better Marketing"
- "10 Killer Content Marketing Concepts for Content Domination"

Now, the final version I choose will be dependent on my keyword and what will most appeal to my readers. Some of these may be too hyperbolic for a more serious audience of, say, savvy business owners new to content marketing. And if my keyword is "content marketing concepts," I would want to prioritize versions where I used the exact-match phrasing. But all this drafting is helping me reach an ultimate understanding of what my final headline needs to do, what words it must contain, and what benefit or outcome I should highlight to best appeal to my audience. The confluence of all those things will result in the best headline possible. So, don't just use the first headline that pops into your brain. Hone that piece of coal into a diamond.

❖ *How to Write a Blog Hook (a.k.a. Introduction)*

Over and over in this book, we've seen a theme emerge: hooks. They're just that important. Almost every piece of online content can include one—and *should* include one, because lighting a spark of interest in your would-be reader is the only way to get them on fire to read your content.

The headline is one piece of your hook. It's a single line that can entice your reader to click your blog link and start reading. But what will keep them reading? The other part of your hook: your blog introduction.

If you're used to writing introductions for school assignments or college essays, you might be taken aback by the differences between those standbys and blog intros. The truth is, they're completely and utterly dissimilar.

Here's what your blog hook/introduction needs to be successful:

- An attention-grabber that's relevant to your topic.
- An answer to the question, "Why should I care?"
- An explanation of what the post will cover/what's to come.
- Smart keyword usage.

Let's look at each of these in detail. We'll use a real-life blog intro example to illustrate concepts. Here it is in its entirety, with the pieces identified in brackets:

INTRODUCTION/HOOK EXAMPLE

[Attention-grabber] We've known for a few years now that content marketing would be worth just over $400

---

billion in 2021. There was no stopping the revolution underway.

And if the research is to be believed, it's going to grow another $269 billion or so by 2024, bringing the total worth to over **$600 billion in 2024.**

[Why should I care?] And guess what the TOP outsourced activity is?

…Content creation.

Among those who outsource, content creation is the activity most outsourced by far.

Content Marketing Activities B2B Organizations Outsource

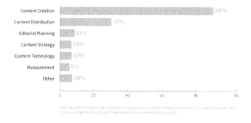

Content marketing has fundamentally changed the way we think about – and create – content online. How we do it today and how we did it ten years ago, when I began, is SO different.

Heck, even ideas that were best practices last year have gone the way of the dust bin.

We're looking at a revolution on par with how Google changed the internet.

[Explanation of what's to come] But why?

Why IS content marketing worth $400 billion?

A lot of people ask me that.

Here's my best take on the phenomenon that is content marketing, and why it's not going away any time soon.

Attention grabber. This is the crux of your hook. This is the thing that should make your reader sit up and pay attention. A good attention-grabber will literally grab them and make it impossible for them to stop reading your blog post.

That doesn't necessarily mean you need to shock them or astound them. It *does* mean you need to give them a reason to care. You can do that by introducing a powerful thought, idea, statistic, or fact that they may not have been aware of, or by pointing out a problem they are currently dealing with relevant to the topic.

In our example, we introduce a powerful thought concerning the worth of the content marketing industry: It's huge, its growth is revolutionary, and it's only going to get bigger, growing to $600 billion in worth by 2024.

Numbers and statistics with big importance to your reader are great to use as your attention-grabber. Power-punching stats can make them sit up and say, "Oh, I should read this." But, the key is to tell your reader WHY those numbers are impactful, HOW the stat may affect them, or WHY it matters in general. That leads us to our next essential element of an introduction/hook.

Why should I care? Don't just hand your reader a problem, idea, thought, stat, or fact and expect them to follow where you're going. Lead them there. Explain why it matters and why they should care. For instance, in the blog intro example, we tell the reader the content marketing industry is expected to balloon to $600B in worth. But WHY does that matter? We tell them: The exploding industry worth is proof of how far content marketing has come; it has fundamentally changed the way we think about marketing and online content. Content marketing is not an option if you want to get known and grow as a business—it's a MUST.

Similarly, if your attention-grabber focuses on stating a problem the reader has now or has had recently, you need to remind them why it matters and what will happen if they don't solve it.

At this point, you may have noticed that we're entirely reader-focused. We keep turning to them to figure out how to frame our introduction and how to hook them. It's all about THEM, not us. If you don't know your audience intimately enough to do this, you'll start to notice as soon as you sit down to write a blog intro.

Explanation of what's to come. Finally, wrap up your introduction and lead into your first main point by previewing what you'll talk about in your blog post. You can give a short summary, a general overview, or talk about a solution if you led with a problem the reader has/is having, which you'll explain more deeply later in the post. Keep it brief, but don't withhold any key information. Get to the point.

In the last few paragraphs of our introduction, we promise our readers that we'll answer a key question (Why is content marketing worth $400B?) and explain why content marketing is a phenomenon that will endure for a long time. Ultimately, including a preview of what's to come at the end of your introduction gives your reader confidence that continuing to read your post will help them meet their goals. And that's exactly what we want.

Smart keyword usage. We've already gone over keyword usage in SEO blogs, but just so you can see this in action, check out the introduction from our example post. The focus keyword is highlighted in yellow, and related keywords are highlighted in blue:

We've known for a few years now that content marketing would be worth just over $400 billion in 2021. There was no stopping the revolution underway.

And if the research is to be believed, it's going to grow another $260 billion or so by 2024, bringing the total worth to over **$600 billion in 2024.**

And guess what the TOP outsourced activity is?

...Content creation.

Among those who outsource, content creation is the activity most outsourced by far.

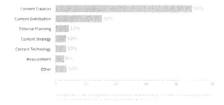

Content Marketing Activities B2B Organizations Outsource

Content marketing has fundamentally changed the way we think about – and create – content online. How we do it today and how we did it ten years ago, when I began, is SO different.

Heck, even ideas that were best practices last year have gone the way of the dust bin.

We're looking at a revolution on par with how Google changed the internet.

But why?

Why IS content marketing worth $400 billion?

A lot of people ask me that.

Here's my best take on the phenomenon that is content marketing, and why it's not going away any time soon.

2. Main Points & Subpoints (Headers and Subheaders)

If you already wrote an outline for your entire blog post, congrats—you skipped ahead of the line. Half the work of writing your headers and subheaders (a.k.a. your main points and subpoints) is done. *Woot!*

But, even if you skipped the outline (I see you, you pantser[26]), you're about to be chagrined because, guess what? You still have to write one.

Yep, you're not dodging that step. Nope, I'm not kidding.

An outline is *essential* for an SEO blog post—indispensable, crucial, a must-have!—because we need that page structure built. It's integral. **Blogs without a good page structure will. Not. Rank.**

So, please. Take a moment to jot down the main points of your blog post. Outline what you'll talk about. Make sure your points are arranged logically, but also ensure their order is engaging. How?

- Arrange your main points in order of importance. The most important information comes FIRST. Don't make your reader scroll through the whole blog just to hunt for the key answer they need.

- If your main points are steps to complete an action, arrange them in the order the reader needs to complete them to accomplish the overarching goal.

Once your points are laid out in the right order, we can move on to tweaking and rewriting your headers and subheaders (a.k.a. your main points and subpoints, H2s and H3s).

---

[26] Pantser: (n) A writer or author who writes without a plan or outline. A pantser literally "flies by the seat of their pants."

There are a few things to think about when we look at perfecting headers, both from an SEO and a writerly standpoint:

How can we cleverly include keywords in the right places?

How can we interest a scanning reader to stop and dive into the text?

How can we keep an engaged reader, well, *reading*?

We can do all of this with descriptive headers—not short, boring ones that contain the bare minimum of information. Let's look at an example to show you what I mean.

Here are all of the headers from a section of our example blog—one H2 plus four H3 subpoints. Note that all of them contain at least two words apiece.

Why Is Content Marketing So Profitable?

1. It's Got a Crazy High ROI

2. It's Future-Proof

3. It's Cheaper than Other Digital Marketing Tactics

4. There's No Talking Without Walking

Image if, instead, these headers were shorter and briefer, like I just copied and pasted my rough blog outline and never bothered to edit them:

"Why Is Content Marketing So Profitable?

1. High ROI

2. Future-Proof

3. Cheaper

4. Hard to Fake"

These are a lot less engaging to read. Why?

They're not conversational. They don't feel like fully-formed thoughts, and they're not direct—who is the writer talking TO, here? We have no idea, and that's a problem because the reader should know you're talking to THEM.

They're devoid of personality. WHO is doing the talking? It could be anyone.

They're not descriptive. For instance, "High ROI" is great, but it's a claim you see all over marketing blogs. The addition of "crazy" adds the descriptive flair it needs to capture attention. Similarly, "Cheaper" lacks oomph when the comparison is incomplete. (Cheaper than what??) And, as for "Hard to Fake," that's a cliché phrase that my eyes skim right over without blinking. On the other hand, "There's No Talking Without Walking" paints a more vivid image, and it makes me want to understand how it relates to content marketing.

They lack keywords. None of the pared-down headers contain keywords that relate to the topic of the post. That's an issue for SEO.

As you can see, headers come alive when we add more descriptive wording. They capture our attention and give us more information and context—and ultimately more understanding of the topic from both a bird's eye view and down in the weeds. That's why, as a general rule, I aim for at least three words or more when I'm writing headers and subheaders. (Bonus: It's easier to include keywords in your headers when they're longer.)

Finally, let's not forget that longer, more descriptive headers are more helpful for the reader skimming your blog. So, when you're composing your H2s and H3s, put yourself in your reader's shoes. Would they understand what your blog is about if they just read the headers? Would they not just get the gist, but the full picture? Would a scanning reader find the information they were searching for? Would your headers pull them down the page, or, better yet, straight into the text? Good headers should do all of those things.

3. Content & Visuals

By now, you have the framework of a post ready and waiting for you to add the bells and whistles. It's time to put up drywall, add windows and doors, paint the walls, and install flooring, staircases, and trim. In other words, it's time to add content and visuals.

First up: content.

When we talk about content, we have to talk about **flow** and **value**.

"Flow" refers to how easy it is to read your content from start to finish. Does one idea lead to the next? When a reader starts reading your blog, do they connect with your words and get carried along on the current of your ideas effortlessly, like a leaf floating down a gentle stream—or is reading your blog like wading through mud?

If you struggle with creating a good flow for readers in your content, try these tips:

Change up your vocabulary. Don't repeat words over and over within the same paragraph. (That's keyword stuffing AND bad writing.) Use synonyms and switch up your verbs and adjectives.

Change up your sentence lengths and structure. Vary your sentences! One of the easiest ways to create a broken flow throughout a piece is to write sentences that all sound the same, with similar lengths.

Use transition words and phrases to link disparate ideas, paragraphs, and sections. Transition words are just words that help connect your sentences, especially when you're shifting from one topic to another or one section to another. Words and phrases like "because," "and," "furthermore," "next," "again," "what's more," "first," "second," "finally," etc. introduce the next thought or idea, transitioning the reader from the previous one. Instead of fast-balling ideas at your audience, lobbing them straight at their faces one after the next, use transitions. These gently pull the reader along your train of thought, which makes for a better reading experience.

Example time.

Don't do this: "Content marketing is profitable because it's hard to fake. That's because content marketing is an incredibly data-driven field. It's hard to make room for guesswork in content marketing."

(All of these sentences are nearly equal in length and sound similar when said aloud. They have roughly the same number of syllables and beats.)

Do this instead: "Content marketing is profitable because it's impossible to fake. Why? It's an incredibly data-driven field. There's no room for guesswork." (This works because I've varied the sentence lengths, and ditched repeating words like "content marketing" and "hard.")

Finally, since this paragraph introduces the last H3 in this section, I can add a transition word to the beginning to ease the reader in and set up their expectations: "**Lastly**, content marketing is profitable because it's hard to fake…"

Once your flow is smoothed out, next you need to think about value.

"Value" refers to what the reader is able to get from reading your content. You should be doing at least one of three things: **educating** them, **informing** them, or **entertaining** them.

- *Educating*: Does the content effectively teach them something so they can learn?

- *Informing*: Does the content provide new knowledge or information the reader has never encountered before?

- *Entertaining*: Does the content make the reader chuckle, does it interest them, or does it actively engage their brain?

Note: Some of the best content does all three at once, but it's very hard to do unless you're an extremely skilled and experienced writer. With that in mind, you don't have to aim for all three simultaneously. But you do need to ensure your content has *at least one* of these value factors.

Now let's look at the flip side. What does it look like when content contains NO value?

- *Boring, lifeless, or dry*: The content has no personality or is written in a way that makes it incredibly boring to read. There's no evidence of the human brand behind the content; anyone (or any bot!) could have written it.

- *Cliché or obvious*: You're not sharing any new information, insights, or ideas. You're regurgitating what already has been said on the topic without putting your spin on it. You're making obvious statements in cliché ways.

- *Poorly explained*: You're sharing new information, but you're presenting it in a way your audience can't latch on to. Your explanations are vague and poorly worded so your readers can't effectively learn from your content.

So, what's the big takeaway, here?

Giving value through content should be unique to your brand and its voice. The *way* you inform, entertain, or educate your audience (or a unique mixture of these three things) is part of your content differentiation factor (CDF).

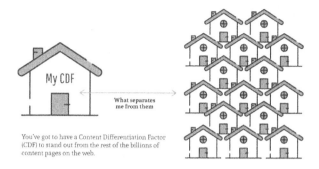

My CDF

What separates
me from them

You've got to have a Content Differentiation Factor
(CDF) to stand out from the rest of the billions of
content pages on the web.

The last point I want to make about giving value in your content is concerned with the reader's primary question: "Why should I care?" Even if they're not aware of it, the reader is *always* in this frame of mind when they read on the web. Their time is limited; their attention span is precious. There are at least 50 other content pieces they could be reading besides yours. So, why should they stay? Why should they spend those minutes with you? *Why should they care?*

Give them reasons throughout your content: **Explain the *why* behind your points.**

In essence, this just means going beyond surface explanations. Don't just offer information; offer information and put it in context. Explain why it matters, why it's relevant to your readers, how it ultimately benefits them, and how it connects to the larger picture. If you can, **include data or statistics** that further back up what you're saying.

Here's an example from our sample blog. The point that "Google expects useful content" is given as one of the reasons why content marketing is worth over $400 billion. But what does useful content have to do with successful content marketing? We tell you why and connect the dots. We know who our reader is and relate to them.

3. Google Expects Useful Content

→ Why should I care?

If you know your SEO history, then you know a lot has changed in the last decade. Namely, Google isn't going to put up with your thin content, your questionable citations, or the fact that you're writing ... ... when you have no business to be doing so.

Google has a vested interest in serving up the best, most useful content it can find. If you don't offer it? You aren't getting to the top of the list.

This is an essential practice to create valuable content.

Now it's time to move beyond the written words in your content piece. It's time to think about **visuals**. Most blogs call for at least one visual somewhere on the page, whether it's an image or photo, an infographic, a gif, or an embedded video.

Visuals enrich your content for a few reasons:

- **They provide a much-needed break for your eyes.** Unbroken paragraphs of text on a screen can be hard to read and may contribute to eye strain (called "computer vision syndrome"[27]).

---

[27] American Optometric Association. (n.d.). "Computer vision syndrome." https://www.aoa.org/healthy-eyes/eye-and-vision-conditions/computer-vision-syndrome

- **They help draw your reader down the page.** Images and visuals are a proven engagement booster. They grab attention and can make your audience keep scrolling. Plus, posts with images are proven to get 2.3x more engagement.[28]

- **They add life and color to your written content.** The power of a great visual can help your readers grasp a difficult concept or visualize what you're saying much better. Visuals can add a whole new layer of meaning if they're well-chosen and relevant to the content.

A few rules for adding visuals to written content like blogs:

- **Don't add a visual just for the sake of adding one**. Instead, make sure it also adds another layer of value to your blog.

- **Look for visuals that help illustrate what you're saying in the text**. Find graphs or charts to help readers visualize statistics and infographics to help them visualize concepts. Add images, photos, and gifs to emphasize a point or bring a description to life. (For example, if I was writing about snowy owls, I would look for images of snowy owls to add to the text.)

- **If you have the resources, invest in original, custom graphics to illustrate your blogs— especially if the concepts are unique to your**

---

[28] BuzzSumo. (2015, May 20). "How to Massively Boost Your Blog Traffic With These 5 Awesome Image Stats." https://buzzsumo.com/blog/how-to-massively-boost-your-blog-traffic-with-these-5-awesome-image-stats/

brand. According to a Venngage survey, original graphics performed the *best* for marketers out of all the visual types.[29] Guess what the worst-performing visuals were? Stock photos.

- **A good rule of thumb**: Add one relevant visual to your content every 200 words.

4. *Calls-to-Action (CTAs)*

CTAs are one of the most underrated parts of SEO blog writing.

Without CTAs, your blog will be useless. People with the problem you target will find your blog, but there will be no way to capture those leads so you can nurture them. That means your audience will read your blog and leave your site, never to be seen or heard from again.

You need a way to direct the traffic and leads your blog will earn from ranking in search. You need to direct them to their next action, AND you need to capture them in some way so they will continue engaging with your brand. Do it with strategic CTAs that lead to an email sign-up page, a lead magnet, or one of your best products/services.

In Content Hacker blogs, we like to end with a soft sell for our free video training. This is a value-packed, on-demand training with me onscreen explaining how to grow a business with content. Now, this ending CTA is a longer one that always appears at the end of the blog

---

[29] Nadya Khoja. (2022, Sept. 26). "16 Visual Content Marketing Statistics to Know for 2022 [Infographic]." Venngage. https://venngage.com/blog/visual-content-marketing-statistics/

conclusion. Note that it blends in seamlessly—we do that by using transition words:

Grow Authority, Not Advertising Spend

It's not hard to see why content marketing is worth $400 billion in 2021. It's a customer-centric, future-proof, data-driven field that's difficult – it not impossible – to fake. I've taken a quick look at what has changed online and why content marketing has become the key strategy for growing your brand online.

> So, what's the next step?   Transition that leads to CTA
>
> Make sure you can walk your talk, of course.
>
> There's never been a better time to invest in content for your business growth...

And I can show you how to do it, step by step, whether you're starting your brand or scaling it up.

It's all inside my Content Transformation System. 📖

This 1:1 coaching program focuses on helping you build a three-fold expertise: business skills, systems, and strategies you can take and apply to your brand immediately.

Read: No more burnout. No more guessing at your next steps. Just clarity, no matter where you stand in your biz-building journey.

Ready to get out of the grunt work and into the delight zone, and build a sustainable business that succeeds? Apply to join my coaching program, the Content Transformation System.

Get a taste of CTS in my free training right here. Sign up to watch instantly.

Then, throughout the rest of the content, we might sprinkle in one or two text or image CTAs to other relevant lead magnets or services. ("Relevant" means we talked about a related topic in the paragraph right before where the CTA appears.)

Remember, natural, relevant CTAs can guide your reader to move further into your sales cycle. They're a key step in ensuring your content is profitable, so always make sure your SEO blogs contain **at least one** CTA to your best product, service, or lead magnet.

5. *Conclusion*

Ready to wrap up this blog with a bang?

Don't trail off without purpose or end abruptly. Instead, tie up your post with a neat bow and include a strong conclusion.

The conclusion is a gift to the reader who stuck around to read your post from beginning to end. It completes your post in a satisfying way. It reiterates the most important points you made, ones you want the reader to remember. And, if you can, you should offer at least one important takeaway or concluding thought for the reader to chew on.

The thing is, millions of useless conclusions already exist out there—don't add yours to the pile. Here are some tips:

- Don't just title this section "Conclusion." Get more creative than that. Instead, try phrasing the section title as an actionable takeaway you want your reader to get from your blog. I.e., in our sample blog, the conclusion section is titled "Grow Authority, Not Advertising Spend."

- Use an H2 for your conclusion heading. Try to include your focus keyword inside the H2.
- Remind your reader of the overarching point you're trying to make in the post. What's the ONE big idea at the heart of it all?
- Reiterate at least one key point that supports your main point.
- Give your reader at least one takeaway to remember from your post. If you could leave them with one parting thought, what would it be? Use your unique perspective to help you out, here.
- Use transition words and phrases to elegantly segue into your final call-to-action.

From Human Content to AI-Assisted Content (AIO): AI + Content Tutorial to 5-10x Your Blog Writing Speed

Once you have all the skills to write a comprehensive, well-structured, keyword-optimized, helpful-for-your-audience SEO blog, you're ready to add an AI writing tool to the mix to streamline your process.

As we discussed in the Preface, this is the future of content creation. If you want to stay ahead of the game you need to figure out how to leverage tools like this in your process. The tool I recommend is called Content at Scale—but there's an entire story about why I'm throwing my weight behind this one. Because remember: I'm one of the biggest AI skeptics out there.

From AI Skeptic to AI Believer

As a writer that believes in the old-fashioned, hard-knocks craft of creating content so good, you "bleed on your typewriter"—I believe Ernest Hemingway himself would be horrified at the butchering of writing that's happening in AI content.

From factual inaccuracy to a complete lack of structure, style, and depth, none of the content from most of the AI tools I tested gave me a real solution for true long-form, which is the content type I teach, preach, study, and practice—to the tune of thousands of blogs written, and over $5M in sales generated for my businesses from the content I write.

For long-form, especially, GPT-3 and its family haven't been a solution in my expert opinion. While ChatGPT writes nice short-form, titles, and recipes, and can even help a non-native writer become adept, it's lacking severely when you try to ask it to produce a 2,000-word blog.

That's why, when I finally found a quality AI content tool that *produces* quality long-form content in January 2023, I jumped forward by leaps and bounds into not only a day-to-day use of their tool, but into their team and a leadership position with them. It all happened so naturally—it was meant to be.

The tool? You've heard me share it in the book already... **Content at Scale. I'm their VP of Marketing, and enjoying every crazy moment**.

That's right. I was so impressed with this tool, its founder, and the company, I agreed to join their team. Particularly, their approach to the problem of factual accuracy in AI content blew me away—they know it's a problem and they're actively working on a solution.

For context, I'd been emailing and talking to the founders of tools, including some of the ones leading the market—I'd even been offered contract work helping them grow!—but I stepped away from all of them after seeing no plan of action for addressing what matters the most in great content: being accurate and integrity-filled in the actual content itself.

So, when I found Content at Scale, I decided to put pedal to the metal—my aggressive writing self cannot help it when I come across an AI writing tool. I emailed Justin McGill, the founder of Content at Scale, and asked him point-blank: "What are you doing for factual accuracy in AI content? This is the main problem I haven't seen anyone solve." I wasn't expecting a great answer.

But the answer surprised me.

Not only was Justin fully transparent about the reality of these tools, telling me: "You'd better check the content in a plagiarism tool"—but, he also said they had a plan for something coming, and the plan was exactly what I would want to see: a feature where the tool would link to credible sources automatically.

That alone made my jaw drop. Gamechanger!

I was instantly intrigued and excited. I booked a call with Justin for January 9th and sent him, that Saturday, a quick game plan on how to grow Content at Scale with an inbound plan. I wanted to work for and with this tool immediately after seeing the big picture of what they were doing, and what they were capable of.

We hopped on a call—jived right away—and I was offered the role of VP of Marketing on the spot.

The reason behind my yes boiled down to several key points: what I'll get to see firsthand by working in their company; the opportunity to work with such an amazing team (seriously, *everyone* is an A-player), and finally, the opportunity to serve with and for a bigger platform (Content at Scale) to share and teach and help the entire content industry adapt, while still retaining ownership of my name and thoughts. I get to lead their content and be a trusted voice in the industry. I get to be a *practitioner.* I get to think of new growth initiatives as I watch the product get better and better and used and loved by thousands of businesses, marketers, and corporations.

As a practitioner, not just a "coach" in name only, I believe I need this experience if I'm meant to continue writing books and launching courses and consulting where I teach and guide you.

Because AI is the future of content creation. We need to adapt or die if we want to keep the jobs we love.

I've chosen my path. What about you?

How to Go From SEO Writer to AIO Writer

This is a big conversation, one that will be hotter and hotter as time goes on.

Once you have the necessary writing expertise, I believe you should make the shift from SEO writer to AIO writer to safeguard your future as the industry adapts to widespread AI use. "AIO" itself is a term that Justin McGill (Content at Scale founder) and I came up with in early January to define the work and process involved around AI-assisted content production. One of my priorities as VP of Marketing at Content as Scale is to help the team come up with models, courses, and training to continue defining the AIO idea as mass use and adaption of AI into content work in general grows like crazy. Marketers and teams *need* a model, a process, to show them exactly how to go from human-only content production to AI-assisted, without losing heart, soul, or brand voice in the process. Enter **AIO.**

What's an AIO writer?

First, "**AIO**" stands for Artificial Intelligence Optimization. This is the process of improving AI content by optimizing it with the expertise of a human trained in SEO and content writing.

That means "**AIO content**" is content produced by an AI (artificial intelligence) AND optimized by a human so it aligns with content goals and reads well for other humans. Because it's supported by AI, you can produce AIO content 5-10x faster than just using human power alone.

And that brings us to "AIO writer."

An **AIO writer** is how you leverage both AI writer tools and human writing expertise. The human AIO writer is well-versed in SEO content and understands how to use a tool like Content at Scale to optimize and edit AI output to ensure the content is relevant, factually accurate, informative, and compelling.

(Remember the issues inherent in using any type of AI writing software? Without a human guiding your tool, you might be left with unoriginal, inaccurate, or robotic-sounding content. No matter how good it is, no AI tool is perfect.)

The bottom line: The help of a solid AI tool allows us to cut the cost, time, and effort SEO content used to require by at least half, if not more. And we do it by giving our writers and content teams an AI baseline to work with.

Hey, you there, the one reading this: THAT'S YOU!

As the future progresses and AI content is more readily adopted, you're going to be the one driving the tools. And, to do that successfully, to create profitable content that appeals to humans, you need a deep well of writing expertise to draw from.

Remember: **Your expertise should drive the tool.** NEVER let a tool create content for you wholesale. Your hand needs to be in the process, steering the ship and tweaking the output so it no longer looks or sounds like *output* (such a clinical word). Instead, under your expert writerly guidance, the *output* should turn into *unique content*.

My tool of choice, Content at Scale, is a mind-blowingly good one—it allows you to generate high-quality content *5-10x faster* than if you did this entirely by hand. The tool also optimizes your entire piece for SEO.

Check out Content at Scale here, along with a full video tutorial from yours truly on how to use it: contenthacker.com/ai

Use this tool to quickly create an incredibly decent first draft. Then, jump into that draft with your writer's pen poised to create magic.

Here's how to get started.

How to Write an SEO Blog 5-10x Faster with AI: Workflow

1. Create a New Project

After you create an account, you'll need to create a project. This is the website you'll be creating content for with Content at Scale.

You'll fill out details like your website name and URL, the purpose of your website/business, your target audience, your preferred tone of voice, and the word count range for your content pieces.

Some great features of CAS are the number of voices it can write in (casual, bold, sarcastic, persuasive, etc.) and the length of the posts it can produce—over 3,000 words!

Once you've added all your details, click "Create Project."

2. Direct Content at Scale to Create Your Content Piece

At his point, you'll be prompted to fill in the details for your new content piece, including the context of the piece and the keyword you want to rank for.

❖ *Keyword*

For best results, do keyword research before diving into Content at Scale. Find a keyword that's both relevant to your audience and easy to rank for (i.e., the KD, or keyword difficulty score, is at 40 or below).

Once you've found a good, relevant keyword, plug it into CAS under "What keyword do you want to rank for?"

❖ *Context*

This is the place where you'll direct CAS on what to write about—in other words, what angles of your topic should it cover? Give the tool initial guidance so it writes on-point content for your keyword and topic.

To figure out the direction your content should take, make sure you research what's ranking at the top of Google already for your keyword. Study the top results and see how they approach the topic. That's a huge clue to the user intent of your keyword, and how you need to write about it to satisfy searchers.

For example, I chose the keyword "improve user experience." Based on what's ranking for that term at the top of Google, I discovered my blog should cover how to use UX, brand design, and copywriting to make a website more engaging and increase conversions.

And that's what I directed CAS to write!

Once you have the direction of your content set, click "Create Content Now."

3. Edit the AI Writer's Output

Now you'll be taken to your project dashboard as Content at Scale works on your content in the background. You should see a screen like this telling you to check back in a few minutes:

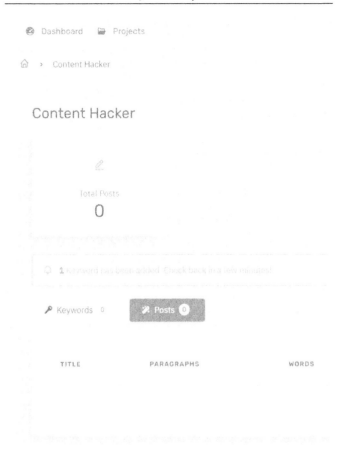

On average, I've found that it takes 10-15 minutes for the tool to create a 2,000+ word post. (Yes—WOW.)

When the post is ready, it will show up in your dashboard like this:

Click on it, and you'll see an editing screen with lots of information. Here's a screenshot overview:

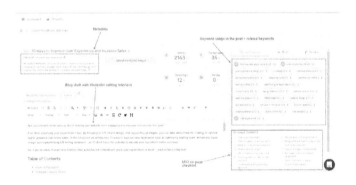

As you can see, this tool is built FOR the SEO content writer. It handles a lot of fussy SEO pieces for you accurately:

- Tracks your keyword usage in the post + suggests related keywords to use.
- Provides an on-page optimization checklist that updates as you go.
- Writes all the metas for you, including a meta description.
- Properly uses keywords in the blog copy.

- Automatically generates a linked table of contents.

Now, you could leave this content as-is and move on to the next step, but I don't recommend that.

What this content is still missing is your personal experience and knowledge—the stuff that can only be found inside YOUR brain.

Content at Scale, or any other AI writing tool, doesn't have access to your memories and knowledge (yet!)—so you need to add your expertise where the copy needs a little zhushing.

You should also edit the post to ensure the flow is good, add internal and external links, insert images, and just generally polish it up so it's even better. Since the quality was already pretty good in the first place, that means you'll be bumping it up to the level of **incredible**, which is powerful.

Follow my **C.R.A.F.T.** checklist to make sure you're editing the content properly (aka, craft better content than AI can by itself):

o **C.** Cut the fluff—ruthlessly. AI is notorious for adding fluff. Remove it.

o **R.** Review and edit (check both grammar and SEO keyword usage; correct, remove, rework and add where necessary).

o **A.** Add media (images, screenshots).

o **F.** Fact-check. Make sure the facts cited are accurate and correct, and link to the source.

o **T.** Build trust (incorporate and add personal story, brand tone, and specific links – i.e. CTAs to your lead magnets, services, etc.).

This step should only take about 30 minutes to 2 hours max, depending on the length and specifics of the piece. For most SEO content writers, who on average can produce a post in 4-6 hours,[30] that adds up to unbelievable time-savings.

❖ *Rerun Post*

Another option for editing the content is to use the "Rerun post" feature. Here's where you'll find it (under the "Brief" tab in the right window):

Click it, and you'll be taken back to the screen where you initially entered your content details. You can tweak these to refine the direction of your content and then rerun the post to produce a tweaked output. You can also click "Customize" in the bottom left corner for even more editing options:

---

[30] Andy Crestodina. (2022). "New Blogging Statistics: What Content Strategies Work in 2022? We asked 1016 Bloggers." Orbit Media Studios. https://www.orbitmedia.com/blog/blogging-statistics

For example, you can edit, add, and rearrange sections. You can even tweak the direction of specific sections. Just remember to hit "Rerun Post" to implement your changes.

4. Run AI Detector and Plagiarism Scans

Once your post is edited and polished, you can run the necessary checks to ensure the content is 100% original and doesn't flag an AI bot detector.

And, you're in luck, because both of these features are built into Content at Scale.

❖ *Plagiarism Scan*

First, up, let's run our completed post through the plagiarism detector hooked up to CAS—Copyscape, a trusted tool.

Navigate to the window on the right side of your content creation dashboard. Click the "Review" tab, then click "Request Plagiarism Scan."

The results will show you what percentage of the text can be found elsewhere online.

If you do get a hit, just rewrite the flagged text.

❖ *AI Detector Scan*

Content at Scale also offers a free AI detector tool.[31] You can run your content through this to check whether your text sounds AI-written.

---

[31] https://contentatscale.ai/ai-content-detector

5. Set Up Importing to WordPress

Last step!

With Content at Scale, you can directly import your finished blog into your WordPress dashboard.

To do this, you need the WordPress plugin, which you can download directly from your CAS dashboard.

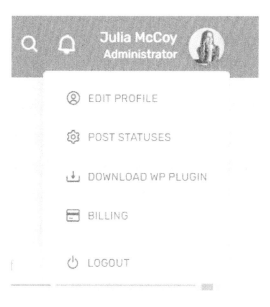

Once that's installed in your WordPress, you can connect Content at Scale by going to your Projects and clicking the three dots by your project name. Click "connect WP" to get an API key that will connect the two services.

Paste the key into the backend of WordPress end to hook the two together.

To make your CAS posts show up in WordPress, you need to have "Pending Editing" enabled as an available post status.

To do that, click the three dots next to your project name and hit "manage settings." Scroll down to the "Post Statuses" section. Click the box under "Select Available Post Status" and select "Pending Editing" in the drop-down menu. This adds it to your post status list.

Then, when you're ready to add your post to WordPress, all you have to do is go to the post status dropdown above the editing screen, change the status to "Pending Editing", and hit "Update."

The post should appear in WordPress in seconds. Voila!

The Question of Copyright for AI-Written Content

One last thing.

Has this question crossed your mind at all?

It certainly never crossed mine until recently.

WHO owns the copyright of content created with an AI tool? (At the end of the day, whose intellectual property is it?)

In the U.K., copyright ownership belongs to the author of the work whether or not they used AI to create it, as you'd expect. But in the U.S., it's not the same. Instead, **in the United States, the copyright of a work produced with AI belongs to the creator of the AI tool**.

This creates some fuzziness, as you'd expect—especially with tools like ChatGPT, which is moving into watermarking content very soon, as well as commercial licensing.[32]

BUT, as long as you're using a tool that gives the copyright back to you, you don't have anything to worry about when you implement AI in your writing process. You will still own the work you create with the help of artificial intelligence.

That *does* mean you need to carefully vet the tool you use. Luckily, **Content at Scale** is one of those tools. The founder, Justin McGill, is ready to hand that copyright straight to you—other tools, not so much. So if you do try other AI content tools, be discerning. The content you create with them might not actually belong to you!

Ready to try Content at Scale? Get started here: contenthacker.com/ai

---

[32] Macie LaCau. (2023, Jan. 5). "OpenAI plans to add watermarking feature to ChatGPT." The American Genius. https://theamericangenius.com/tech-news/chatgpt-watermark/

Checklist for SEO Blog Writing

Headers:

o A winning SEO blog post has a **structure** with strategic headers, nested correctly. *AI Tip: Use Content at Scale to do this FOR YOU.*

o Use your headers **to help the reader** scan, navigate, and understand your post. *AI Tip: Use Content at Scale to do this FOR YOU.*

o Make your headers descriptive and use keywords inside them. *AI Tip: Use Content at Scale to do this FOR YOU.*

Keyword Usage:

o Always place keywords in your title/headline, meta description, intro paragraph, and H2s and H3s. *AI Tip: Use Content at Scale to do this FOR YOU.*

o In the content itself, don't overcomplicate keyword usage! Above all, aim to be helpful to your readers and relevant to your topic. The keywords should naturally fall into place.

Writing the Blog:

o Smart writers always outline their SEO blog posts, first. This outline will serve as the foundational structure of the content. (Structure. Is. Vital!) *AI Tip: Use Content at Scale to do this FOR YOU.*

o As you write, always try to be answering the underlying reader question: "Why should I care?"

o Pay attention to the flow of your content. Try to give your audience the easiest reading experience possible. Use transition words and phrases to guide them through your points and ideas.

o Include relevant visuals every 200 words to increase engagement.

o Always include at least one relevant call-to-action that directs readers to your best lead magnet, product, or service.

o Always wrap up your post. Add a valuable conclusion at the end with key takeaways for the reader.

Editing AI Output:

Never, ever publish straight from tool to site, unless you want to get in serious trouble with factual inaccuracy, lack of tone and humanity, stale content... that list goes on and on. Once you get writing output from an AI tool (i.e. Content at Scale), follow my **C.R.A.F.T.** checklist to craft beautiful content from AI output:

o **C.** Cut the fluff—ruthlessly. AI is notorious for adding fluff. Remove it.

○ **R.** Review and edit (check both grammar and SEO keyword usage; correct, remove, rework and add where necessary).

○ **A.** Add media (images, screenshots).

○ **F.** Fact-check. Make sure the facts cited are accurate and correct, and link to the source.

○ **T.** Build trust (incorporate and add personal story, brand tone, and specific links – i.e. CTAs to your lead magnets, services, etc.).

SEO Blog Writing Outline

1. **Headline + hook** – "hook" is your intro paragraph (under 300 words)
   - Include statements to address pain points and how you'll solve them inside the blog
2. **Summary content** (usually to introduce the points under the coming H3s)
   - First CTA can go here
3. **Subheaders & content**
   - Create your first point that leads the guide or guided points within the article.
4. **Further content & supporting visuals**
   - 1 visual every 200w
   - Optimize with natural usage of focus keyword & secondary keywords
   - (Repeat 3 & 4 as necessary. Optimize with natural usage of focus keyword)
5. **Conclusion (H2)** - include focus keyword
   - End in a soft sell (up to 4-5 sentences or 3 paras) + **CTA** that goes to your best landing page/sales page

AIO WRITER'S CHECKLIST:
C-R-A-F-T Better Content

Once you get writing output from an AI tool (i.e. Content at Scale), follow this checklist for editing success:

C. = Cut the fluff—ruthlessly. AI is notorious for adding fluff. Remove it.

R. = Review and edit (check both grammar and SEO keyword usage; correct, remove, rework and add where necessary).

A. = Add media (images, screenshots).

F. = Fact-check. Make sure the facts cited are accurate and correct, and link to the source.

T. = Build trust (incorporate and add personal story, brand tone, and specific links – i.e. CTAs to your lead magnets, services, etc.).

CHAPTER 5:

Sales Page Writing

Sales pages are where some serious magic happens.

Think of these pages—where you explain your product or service to your customer and try to get them to buy—as the summit of the mountain.

When your prospects reach this peak, that means they've already taken a journey with you along winding paths of content published on your blog, in your emails, on your social media feeds, and more. You've led them this far successfully. They're familiar with you, their sherpa, and they have some trust in you. When they finally follow you to the mountaintop of your sales page, that means they're ready to plant their flag in your brand's soil and *commit*.

You just need to give them one final boost so they can reach the tippy-top and look out over the magnificent view.

That's your sale.

However, although we do want to encourage the prospect to buy, though we do want to nudge them toward the sale, *we never want to seem physically pushy*. Pushiness and over-the-top salesiness ultimately lead to sleaziness. If you push too far with your pitch, or make audacious claims (i.e.,"Make $1 million in 30 days with this strategy!" Or, "I have the ONLY secret you ever need!") buyers will feel coerced or manipulated, which is never what we want. Why? Those feelings **break trust permanently**, and you'll never see that prospect again.

Though by this point I possibly sound like a song played on repeat, the best way to sell through content writing is through offering value, empathizing with your reader's deepest problems, and offering solutions with proof that they work. Think gentle nudges and encouragement, NOT strong pushes and coercion.

If you're leery of sales page writing (especially considering how tough it is to get right), I don't blame you. But, I'm here to tell you that **you can do this**. Just like every other type of content writing, a good sales page can be constructed with a formula we can tweak for anything you want to sell. From *years* of studying the best sales page writers and perfecting my own formula, I've got the "how-to" in my back pocket—and I'm keen to share it with you.

First, a few notes on sales page writing.

A Few Notes and Tips for Writing Effective Sales Pages

Long-Form Wins…

There's a reason why most sales pages you see on the web are long-form. More copy gives you more space to overcome the reader's objections to making a purchase.

For example, an incredibly successful sales page writer and conversion copywriter, Joanna Wiebe of Copyhackers, regularly uses long-form content to sell courses. This page selling a $500 program, in particular, is about 3,000 words long:

10xemails.com/get-it-now

Yep, it's extensive…

…But, more importantly, every inch of this copy is *good*.

And that's what matters, even more than its length.

No matter what kind of content we're talking about, length matters. Learn more, including how to determine the right length for your content:
contenthacker.com/blogging-length

That leads me to my next tip for effective sales pages.

…But Don't Go Overboard

Yes, while the above sales page is as long as a lazy and uneventful Saturday, while the copy is plentiful, **none of it is fluff, and no space is wasted**.

You heard me: NO FLUFF.

If you veer off into fluff-land and waste your prospect's time with stuff they don't care about, your sales page won't be a sales page—it will be a black hole where potential customers disappear, never to be seen again.

We're not making a sales page long for the sake of length; we're making it long because we have so much important information to share with our reader. That includes our value proposition (how the prospect will benefit from the offer), explaining the offer (who it's for, who it's not for), proof that our offer delivers (re: testimonials), why we're passionate about delivering our offer, overcoming objections to the offer, etc. etc. (we'll discuss the full formula in a second).

For this reason, commit to length for your sales pages, but don't go overboard. I recommend **3,000-3,500 words, max**. Go long, but simultaneously cut the fluff, refine, edit, and hone your copy so absolutely no space is wasted and every word helps your prospect move toward the sale.

Feel Free to Tinker with the Structure Without Removing Key Pieces

Rules were meant to be broken, especially when you're a confident, creative writer who knows them inside and out. That's why, once you fully understand the structure of a successful sales page, you should feel free to play around with the flow and order of sections, rearranging, merging, and tweaking as you see fit. Your gut as a writer should absolutely guide you—just don't remove any pieces altogether. As you'll soon find out, each piece of the sales page formula plays a vital role in the overall success of the content.

Use AI In Your Sales Copywriting Process

Tools like Jasper, Copy, Copymatic, Anyword, heck—even our own, Content at Scale—can help you generate an efficient starting point for your sales page. I highly recommend using it in the **blank draft process**—remember our writer's hat idea:

The writer's hat material

Read Every Day

Use AI to dramatically reduce blank-page syndrome

Invest in Yourself

What Happened When I Tried to Generate a Sales Page with ChatGPT and Jasper

I gave Jasper and ChatGPT the same prompt: *Create a sales page for a new upcoming Content Hacker course that will help business owners learn how to write AI-assisted blog content and grow their businesses.* Here's what it did:

Jasper doesn't have a ton of long-form options (really, any, if you try to get them to write 2,500+ words): but it does have the classic **AIDA** marketing framework:

AIDA Framework
Use the oldest marketing framework in the world. Attention, Interest, Desire, Action.

Company/Product name   14/80

  Content Hacker

Product description   162/800

  Create a sales page for a new upcoming Content Hacker course that will help business owners learn how to write AI-assisted blog content and grow their businesses.

Tone of voice   21/80

  Practical and Helpful

I gave it the prompt above, and here's what it generated:

> Attention: Learn how to write AI-assisted blog content that will help you grow your business!
>
> Interest: Content Hacker is excited to offer a new course that will teach business owners how to take advantage of artificial intelligence in their writing. You'll learn how to produce more engaging and effective blog content with the help of AI.
>
> Desire: In today's digital age, it's more important than ever to have an effective online presence. With this new course from Content Hacker, you'll be able to write content that stands out from the competition and helps you reach your business goals.
>
> Action: Sign up for our new course today and start writing better blog content tomorrow!

Not bad for some baseline content to work with, but also—not very good. There's fluff here, absolutely zero unique information, and a complete lack of long-form.

I asked ChatGPT the same thing, and here's what it gave me:

Create a sales page for a new upcoming Content Hacker course that will help business owners learn how to write AI-assisted blog content and grow their businesses.

Introducing the Content Hacker Course: Unleash the Power of AI-Assisted Blogging

Are you a business owner who wants to grow your online presence and attract more customers through content marketing? Do you struggle with creating engaging and high-quality blog posts that drive traffic and conversions? Look no further! The Content Hacker Course is here to help you take your content marketing game to the next level.

With this comprehensive online course, you'll learn how to harness the power of AI-assisted blogging to produce top-notch content that engages your audience, boosts your search engine ranking, and drives business growth. Whether you're a seasoned blogger or just starting out, our expert instructors will guide you through the entire process of creating high-performing content with the help of cutting-edge AI technology.

What You'll Learn:

* The basics of AI-assisted content creation and how it can benefit your business
* How to conduct keyword research and identify popular topics to write about
* Techniques for writing captivating headlines and body content that resonates with your target audience
* How to optimize your blog posts for search engines and increase your visibility

* Best practices for using AI tools to enhance your content quality and productivity

With our step-by-step video lessons, interactive quizzes, and hands-on projects, you'll gain the skills and confidence you need to write blog posts that get results. You'll also have access to a supportive community of fellow business owners and content marketers, where you can exchange ideas, get feedback, and build lasting relationships.

Don't wait any longer to start creating powerful and effective content that grows your business. Enroll in the Content Hacker Course today and discover the secrets to writing blog posts that engage and convert.

Sign up now and take the first step towards content marketing success!

Not bad! There's a hook, summary, a *What You'll Learn* section, and a pretty strong wrap-up to the end. I can work with this.

What Happened When I Asked Content at Scale to Write a Long-Form Sales Page

Content at Scale isn't built for sales copy—but, the internal machine is so good at writing, we've found that it writes pretty darn good promotional copy. So, I tasked it with the same exact prompt I gave Jasper and ChatGPT. I really liked the headline it generated:

Level Up Your Business With an AI Writing Course!
Target Keyword: AI writing course - 02-06-2023 04:38 AM

I would probably change that to be more targeted to my end user, i.e. Level Up Your Writing Skills by Becoming an AI Writer: The Step-By-Step Course or something like that (since I'm targeting writers here). *But,* this gave me phrasing ideas, i.e. Level Up—which really help me get going.

I was pleasantly surprised by the meta description and first paragraph (hook)—pretty darn good.

"Are you an entrepreneur looking to leverage the power of AI Writing for your business? With our new Content Hacker course, we can show you how.

From best practices on creating quality content with AI writing to tips for measuring success, this AI writing course is designed specifically to help business owners get ahead.

Our expert team will provide insights and advice that no other ai writing courses offer. Sign up now and learn how AI Writing can transform your website into one that drives growth and scale in 2023."

I can work with that sales copy! It's strong, succinct, and powerful. (Just needs to be targeted to writers—it's currently speaking to the wrong audience.)

The rest of the article, true-to-form, is a blog. I had to chuckle because just like a blog would, it recommends a course it found (this course won't help AI writers at all—it's a techy course, more suited for AI engineers):

versions of the same piece, allowing them to test different approaches and find the best fit for their audience. Additionally, AI-powered grammar checkers are useful for catching typos and other errors that may have been missed by human editors. Finally, AI-based summarization tools can help writers condense large amounts of information into shorter pieces without sacrificing quality or accuracy.

Is AI writing free?

No, AI writing is not free. AI writing services typically require a subscription fee or pay-per-use model in order to access their features and tools. Depending on the specific service, fees can range from a few dollars per month to hundreds of dollars per month. Additionally, some AI writing services may require additional fees for certain features or access to higher quality content.

What is the best course to learn AI?

The best course to learn AI is the Artificial Intelligence Nanodegree program from Udacity. This comprehensive program covers the fundamentals of AI, including deep learning, computer vision, natural language processing and more. It also provides hands-on projects and real-world case studies to help you apply your knowledge in a practical setting. The program is designed for both beginners and experienced professionals who want to take their skillset to the next level. With expert instructors guiding you through each step of the way, this nanodegree will equip you with all the necessary tools needed to become an AI master.

Conclusion

In conclusion, AI Writing is a powerful tool that can help business owners create quality content quickly and efficiently. With the right strategies and techniques, you can leverage this technology to grow your business and reach new heights of success. The Content Hacker AI Writing Course will provide you with all the necessary tools to make the most out of this amazing technology. Sign up today for our upcoming course and learn how to use AI writing to its fullest potential.

So, a bit off for sales copy, but we have the start of something amazing to work with here.

Final Thoughts on AI + Sales Copy

When it comes to publishing the sales page, never publish straight from the AI tool without serious editing. In fact, sometimes you'll find you need to do a lot of work to get it publish-ready. Sales pages are *extra* tricky because you want them to, well, convert. That requires the right formula and the right pieces in the right places. So, you'll want to fine-tooth comb it and make sure all fifteen points in the sales page formula (below) are inside the content written by AI.

Pssst… The first step to becoming a Content Hacker-level content creator is getting on my list. Get first access to our content right when it drops, plus videos, freebies, and tips for perfecting your business and content marketing skills when you sign up for emails: contenthacker.com/subscribe

My 15-Point Sales Page Formula, Broken Down

Here's an overview of the formula you're about to learn:

1. Hook
2. Details
3. Urgency
4. Proof
5. What It's Not/What It Is
6. Who It's For/Not For
7. New Paradigm/Original Concept
8. How You Learned
9. How It's Working
10. Time Is of the Essence (Again)
11. Why Are We Doing This?
12. Paint the Future & Overcome Obstacles
13. What to Do Right Now
14. CTA—Let's Talk
15. Guarantee & FAQs
16. Bonus: Repel

Each point in this formula is necessary to construct your sales page. Remember, you can move any of these pieces around to fit your needs—you can even combine multiple together in one—but you shouldn't delete any of them. And, of course, the hook needs to be the first piece—don't mess with that in the order. Let's start there.

1. Hook

By now, you know that a hook is an attention-grabber, an interest-earner, an eye-catcher. It snares your reader and pulls them deeper into your copy. Ultimately, it's what keeps them reading your sales page.

For this formula, the hook refers to up to three pieces of copy:

1. The headline
2. The sub-headline
3. The intro copy

One of the keys to constructing a successful hook is **specificity**. You need to tell the reader EXACTLY what they can expect to get out of your offer in terms of **benefits** and **value**. You should answer these questions with your hook:

- WHAT problem are you solving for the customer?
- HOW does your solution benefit them?
- WHAT are the potential positive outcomes of buying?
- WHY are you/the brand the best provider of this solution?

Here's an example of a hook from the sales page for my coaching program, The Content Transformation System:

Headline: "A Step-by-Step Program for Creative Founders to (Entirely) Skip the Burnout and Sustainably Grow a 7-Figure Brand"

Sub-headline: "Skills, strategy and systems—all you need to grow sustainably. Work with Julia and our trained Content Hacker coaches, and our immersive training pathway. Get started for as little as $9/day."

To make it easier on yourself, consider using this framework for your headline: "Learn how to [outcome 1], [outcome 2], and [outcome 3]."

See how my example headline fits this mold? "A Step-by-Step Program for Creative Founders [learn how] to (Entirely) Skip the Burnout [outcome 1] and Sustainably Grow a 7-Figure Brand [outcome 2]."

Remember *specificity*. Call out the exact audience you're targeting and tell them exactly what they'll get out of the offer in terms of value for their lives. Think bigger than the product or service at face value—what are the **intangible benefits** of buying, the ones that will show up as a result of using the product/service and change the buyer's life for the better?

By the way, as we examine each piece of a winning sales page, I'll show you the corresponding section from a real-life sales page. When we reach the end, I'll put the entire puzzle together with all the parts connecting so you can see the whole picture. Here's the hook from our main example:

UNLEARN ESSAY WRITING: YOUR PROFESSIONAL ONLINE WRITING COURSE

Become an expert web content writer. Learn how to write for all formats, and receive in-depth mentorship & critique on your writing from our expert coaches.

> ## HOOK - EXAMPLE:
>
> **Unlearn Essay Writing: Your Professional Online Writing Course**
> Become an expert web content writer. Learn how to write for all formats, and receive in-depth mentorship & critique on your writing from our expert coaches.

2. Details (Describe Yourself/the Brand + a Summary of the Offer)

Here's your first opportunity for storytelling on your sales page. (As we know, stories attract human interest like nothing else. Tell stories on your page related to the offer, and you'll engage much better.)

First off, describe who you (or the brand) are. What's the backstory behind how you/the company came to be, and ultimately how you came to sell XYZ? Furthermore, what's your big WHY behind what you do? Why are you offering this product/service, ultimately? What overarching problem are you aiming to solve with your business?

Along with offering an engaging story, this section also provides some proof that you're legit and are the best option for the customer. You can share a bit of history, your wins in your industry, and why you (or the brand) are considered an expert on the particular problem the offer solves.

To see this section in action, take a look at our example of a real-life sales page:

Hi, I'm Julia McCoy, and I've Been Teaching Writers to Unlearn the Essay Writing Habit for Nearly a Decade.

Nine years ago, I started my content agency Express Writers from scratch.

What I had then:

- $75 in my pocket
- No support system
- My passion for writing and dream to someday make a living doing what I love

What we have now:

- A growing brand worth $5 million
- 90 expert writers, content strategists, QA professionals, and blog editors
- 1,300 blogs published
- 20,000 successfully completed projects

The #1 asset that got me from what I had THEN to what I have NOW?

Great content.

And I mean to continue the trend. In fact, I personally sift through the bulk of writer applicants I get each week (and hire only 1% of them). Out of the bigger group, I cultivate a small team that writes personally for me.

Since 2011, I've worked with my team of writers, first to help them **"unlearn" the bad essay habits** their college professor taught them and then to **learn the art of creating top-notch content.**

Because yes, even the best writers I've worked with carry around a chunk of this bad habit in their systems.

After nine years of intensive training experience, I've come up with: **a polished system that gets writers from producing chunky, fluff-filled writing to engaging, fun, in-demand content.**

And I don't mean to keep this system to myself. It's high time every wishful writer had their hands on a training that's actionable.

DETAILS - EXAMPLE:

Hi, I'm Julia McCoy, and I've Been Teaching Writers to Unlearn the Essay Writing Habit for Nearly a Decade.

Nine years ago, I started my content agency Express Writers from scratch.
What I had then:
- $75 in my pocket
- No support system
- My passion for writing and dream to someday make a living doing what I love

What we have now:
- A growing brand worth $5 million
- 90 expert writers, content strategists, QA professionals, and blog editors
- 1,300 blogs published
- 20,000 successfully completed projects

The #1 asset that got me from what I had THEN to what I have NOW?

Great content.

And I mean to continue the trend. In fact, I personally sift through the bulk of writer applicants I get each week (and hire only 1% of them). Out of the bigger group, I cultivate a small team that writes personally for me.

Since 2011, I've worked with my team of writers, first to help them **"unlearn" the bad essay habits** their college professor taught them and then to **learn the art of creating top-notch content**.

Because yes, even the best writers I've worked with carry around a chunk of this bad habit in their systems.

After nine years of intensive training experience, I've come up with: **a polished system that gets writers from producing clunky, fluff-filled writing to engaging, fun, in-demand content.**

And I don't mean to keep this system to myself. It's high time every wishful writer had their hands on a training this actionable.

3. Urgency (Why They Should Buy Now)

Urgency gives the sales page you're writing a little zip behind it. You want to light a fire behind the prospects reading this page, providing them with an even greater reason to act (re: buy).

Now, there's a slimy way to do this and a smart way. The slimy way involves making your prospect feel rushed, anxious, and fearful. The **smart** way doesn't invoke any anxiety, but rather makes them feel like it would be a *better idea* to buy now versus later. There are a few ways to accomplish this.

- **Provide an end date for a good deal**: For example, you could offer a reduced price if your prospect buys now. Tell them exactly when the deal goes away to produce urgency.
  - **Example**: "60% off ends in 4 days."
- **Limited time to buy/waitlist**: Tell customers that buying/enrolling/etc. is only open for a short amount of time. Mention the possibility of being waitlisted if they don't buy now.

- o **Example**: "We've had to open and close this program over the last few months because it's been so effective and we simply can't help a thousand people at a time… hurry before we move to a waiting list."
- **Speak directly to their greatest pain point**: For this method, you don't need to mention end dates, waitlists, timers, or discounts. Simply speaking to and solving their greatest pain is impetus enough to move them forward.
    - o **Example**: "Growing your business strategically and sustainably to 7 figures isn't guesswork. It isn't luck either. Or about being a special type of person, having a ton of capital, or having decades of experience. Nope. You can be a beginner who just went all-in on your business idea. Or you can be a struggling entrepreneur with years of trying behind you. And you can make it. You can grow your business to whatever you desire it to be… in just 90 days of learning, with The Content Transformation System."

Here's how we included urgency on our real-life sales page:

What if you could learn the professional writing skills used by TOP-NOTCH content creators in just one week?

Does this sound like you?

You're in the world of online content. Maybe suddenly. Maybe you've planned for it.

You're writing content, and you're getting your feet wet.

The HUGE fear in your gut: you don't have the actual **skill of writing for the web** down pat.

Sure, you've blogged maybe once or twice, but it's been as a passion or a hobby.

You were trained academically... not for this online stuff.

But, you won at English in school. Maybe in college, your professor gave you STRAIGHT A's for your essays.

So why are you getting the feeling that your college degree wasn't for this new world of online writing?

Hint: You're right.

In fact, I say the essay writing style you learned in college is the #1 **bad habit** keeping you from the explosive online writing career of your dreams. And that's what I'm here to help you **kick for good**, before teaching you how to write for the web and frame the top 11 formats, in Unlearn Essay Writing.

Enroll Now

URGENCY - EXAMPLE:

What if you could learn the professional writing skills used by TOP-NOTCH content creators in just one week?

Does this sound like you?

You're in the world of online content. Maybe suddenly. Maybe you've planned for it.

You're writing content, and you're getting your feet wet.

The HUGE fear in your gut: you don't have the actual **skill of writing for the web** down pat.

Sure, you've blogged maybe once or twice, but it's been as a passion or a hobby.

You were trained academically... not for this online stuff.

But, you won at English in school. Maybe in college, your professor gave you STRAIGHT A's for your essays.

So why are you getting the feeling that your college degree wasn't for this new world of online writing?

Hint: You're right.

In fact, I say the essay writing style you learned in college is the **#1 bad habit** keeping you from the explosive online writing career of your dreams. And that's what I'm here to help you **kick for good,** before teaching you how to write for the web and frame the top 11 formats, in Unlearn Essay Writing.

4. Proof

How do you continue building trust on a sales page? After all, this *whole thing* is an exercise in trust. You're ultimately capitalizing on trust built over time with the prospect reading the page (because they found the offer through the brand's other content!), but you also need to take what's there and ratchet it up to a crescendo if you want the sale once the prospect has finished reading.

How? To continue building trust, you need to provide further proof the brand is trustworthy—but not from the brand's mouth.

Now is the time to pull out testimonials from previous happy customers and display them prominently on your sales page.

No testimonials yet from people who have purchased the offer? Related testimonials from people who have worked with the brand in some way are good, too.

What Students Say About Julia's Unlearn Essay Writing Course

5. *What It Is/What It's Not*

As we keep moving through the formula, some sections, like this one, are all about continuing to clarify your offer so there's zero uncertainty about what it is/what it includes/what it does NOT include.

Take the opportunity here to summarize your offer in the clearest terms possible, including what it is NOT about.

Example: "This is not a get-rich-quick scheme… it only works for *legitimate* experts (nurses, doctors, skilled trades, professional writers, authors, coaches with proven track records, etc.)."

In our real-life example, we wrote a short section dedicated to describing exactly what the offer (a course) is about:

Grow Your Content Writing Skills & Get Paid to Write

In **The Unlearn Essay Writing Course, I help freelancers learn how to write for the web, so they can build confidence for and real skills in content creation**. Learn how to write for the top 11 content formats, and

---

WHAT IT IS/WHAT IT'S NOT - EXAMPLE:

Grow Your Content Writing Skills & Get Paid to Write

In **The Unlearn Essay Writing Course, I help freelancers learn how to write for the web, so they can build confidence for and real skills in content creation**. Learn how to write for the top 11 content formats, and create content with confidence.

---

6. Who It's For/Not For

In this section, you'll quickly reinforce #5 (what it is/isn't) with a summary of **who** the offer is for, and who it isn't for. This helps further qualify prospects and will turn away anyone who doesn't fit the mold (which is good—those people weren't going to buy, anyway). Even better, it will help further convince someone on the fence, who isn't sure the offer is for them, when they see themselves described.

This piece is so simple, it's best explained by example:

Who Is The Unlearn Essay Writing Course For?

B2Bs and B2Cs: Reach your ideal partners and clients with professionally-written emails, case studies, white papers, and more.

Entrepreneurs: Engage your audience like never before with compelling content they can't resist.

Brands: With 7+ billion daily searches on Google, there's no better place to shape your brand than online. The best way to do it? With engaging, compelling creative content.

Freelancers: Stand head and shoulders above your competition with writing skills high-paying clients are looking for.

Service-Based Businesses and Providers: Showcase your services and out-class your competition with value-rich content.

All Industries: The content writing skills I teach in this course apply to you no matter what kind of product or service you offer (or even if you don't offer a product or service, but just want to gain a following online for fun!)

WHO IT'S FOR/NOT FOR - EXAMPLE:

Who Is The Unlearn Essay Writing Course For?

B2Bs and B2Cs: Reach your ideal partners and clients with professionally-written emails, case studies, white papers, and more.

Entrepreneurs: Engage your audience like never before with compelling content they can't resist.

Brands: With 7+ billion daily searches on Google, there's no better place to shape your brand than online. The best way to do it? With engaging, compelling, creative content.

Freelancers: Stand head and shoulders above your competition with writing skills high-paying clients are looking for.

Service-Based Businesses and Providers: Showcase your services and outshine your competitors with value-rich content.

All industries: The content writing skills I teach in this course apply to you no matter what kind of product or service you offer (or even if you don't offer a product or service, but just want to gain a following online for fun!)

7. New Paradigm/Original Concept

Next up: Present your offer in the context of how original it is, or how it leans on a new, innovative way of thinking that supercedes old methods and/or beliefs. Compare/contrast the old with the new, and, if applicable, provide data on why the old ways are outdated (remember, your audience needs proof that your offer works, and they need to hear it from other sources, not just your mouth).

In my example sales page, we present the offer (enrollment in my Unlearn Essay Writing course) in direct opposition to an old standard of writing—academic/essay writing. Unlearn Essay Writing literally teaches you to *unlearn* everything you learned about writing in school. That's because stuffy, academic writing doesn't work in the online content world, where we're trying to engage readers, hold their interest, and present them with solutions to their questions and problems.

See how that works? My offer is framed as the new paradigm with academic writing as the outdated one, and this contrast sets us up to appear innovative, original, and forward-thinking, which is incredibly persuasive.

NEW PARADIGM/ORIGINAL CONCEPT - EXAMPLE

Sure, you've blogged maybe once or twice, but it's been as a passion or a hobby.

You were trained academically… not for this online stuff.

But, you won at English in school. Maybe in college, your professor gave you STRAIGHT A's for your essays.

So why are you getting the feeling that your college degree wasn't for this new world of online writing?

Hint: You're right.

In fact, I say the essay writing style you learned in college is the **#1 bad habit** keeping you from the explosive online writing career of your dreams. And that's what I'm here to help you **kick for good,** before teaching you how to write for the web and frame the top 11 formats, in Unlearn Essay Writing.

---

8. *How You Learned*

How did you learn to find the depth of knowledge you have now? How did you gain your expertise (or how did the brand grow to become an authority)? What was the journey from point A to point B? Tell that story on your sales page—however briefly you want. Include details and data, like how many clients you've served (or the brand has served) since you started, what you've been able to accomplish for them, and how that ties back into the offer.

For example, you can keep it to one paragraph, like: "In 2016, I took my first client as a content writer after years spent writing papers for my Master's degree, not to mention fiction and short stories as a hobby. I earned pennies per word and loved every second. Soon, I was helping dozens of clients write engaging web content that resulted in leads, clicks, sales, and loyal followings. And now I'm taking that knowledge into our Content Writing Service."

Note: This piece of the puzzle naturally lends itself to being combined with the "Details" piece. Use your discretion and look at your sales page as a whole to determine if that's a good idea. Make sure you aren't repeating yourself needlessly in each section. In fact, if that's what's happening, it's a good sign you should combine the two.

Here's another example from our real-life sales page (as you'll note, we did in fact embed this part into our "Details" section):

HOW YOU LEARNED - EXAMPLE
Nine years ago, I started my content agency from scratch. What I had then: • $75 in my pocket • No support system • My passion for writing and dream to someday make a living doing what I love

What we have now:
- A growing brand worth $5 million
- 90 expert writers, content strategists, QA professionals, and blog editors
- 1,300 blogs published
- 20,000 successfully completed projects

The #1 asset that got me from what I had THEN to what I have NOW?

Great content.

9. How It's Working

Continue the above story and reinforce how what you/the brand is doing now is exponentially working—not just for you, but for others, too. In this section, you can add case studies or testimonials of your (or the brand's) success.

A case study told in story form is incredibly compelling, here. Don't just list numbers or data you tracked; explain the problem your customer/client faced, explain how that affected them, and then explain how your solution solved it, including how it benefitted the client in ways beyond the obvious.

On our real sales page, we told the story of a writer I guided to "unlearn" the essay writing habit to *show* how the methods I use and teach in the course work.

Erin's Journey: How She Unlearned the Essay Writing Habit...and Got Paid to Write

Erin is part of my small team of personal writers – the writers who create content for my brands.

She's a history graduate with a natural passion for writing. Like me, she's loved writing since she was 12! (Natural passion is a GREAT place to start from as a writer.)

Once Erin passed our writer tests, she was ready to take on her first assignment.

The topic? A blog on UX writing.

After she'd written it, she uploaded it for me to read. I opened up the document and read this:

"UX has become an extremely relevant topic in recent years, but it is a field that is still somewhat obscure and unknown as it is still early in its growth. Nonetheless, it is clear that this field is quickly becoming an important area of focus for business, and so there is a lot of potential in this industry."

I recognized it the moment I saw it.

The essay writing habit.

HOW IT'S WORKING - EXAMPLE

Erin is part of my small team of personal writers – the writers who create content for my brands.

She's a history graduate with a natural passion for writing. Like me, she's loved writing since she was 12! (Natural passion is a GREAT place to start from as a writer.)

Once Erin passed our writer tests, she was ready to take on her first assignment.

The topic? A blog on UX writing.

After she'd written it, she uploaded it for me to read. I opened up the document and read this:

"UX has become an extremely relevant topic in recent years, but it is a field that is still somewhat obscure and unknown as it is still early in its growth. Nonetheless, it is clear that this field is quickly becoming an important area of focus for business, and so there is a lot of potential in this industry."

I recognized it the moment I saw it.

The essay writing habit.

I knew I'd have to guide Erin like I'd guided dozens before her. And I did. I helped her "unlearn" the essay writing habit and replace it with the skills and techniques I used to build my brand.

Two assignments later, I was reading this:

"Think of your business as a restaurant. You are the chef, and your role is to produce great food (content) that they will love. …Now that you have the four-step recipe for getting past your inner critic to content that matters, you're ready to publish great material."

Massive improvement. Erin now earns a paycheck, doing what she loves – starting with being on my agency payroll! Going from stuffy to savvy — from bland and boring to a banquet of rich, engaging content — is **not** easy.

And it takes a mentor to know how to go about doing this, if you don't have the slightest clue.

Till now, I've only done this training internally with my top writers. And it takes them to a place of consistent revenue, where they're earning assignments EVERY week. Today, I'm opening up this training to you, in this exclusive training course.

10. Time Is of the Essence (Again)

It's important to emphasize the urgency behind the offer (in a non-sleazy way). Do this by mentioning, again, how important/beneficial acting now will be for your prospect. This can look as simple as a line of text with a CTA underneath it, or it can be a line added to the end of one of the above sections. If you can, mention time in some way (e.g., "right now," "don't miss out," "it's time," "until now," etc.) to give that nudge to the reader to remind them that they **don't** have all the time in the world to decide whether to buy.

Example: "Till now, I've only done this training internally with my top writers. And it takes them to a place of consistent revenue, where they're earning assignments EVERY week. Today, I'm opening up this training to you, in this exclusive training course."

On our real-life sales page, we included this text + CTA in the middle of the sales page, and it also serves to create that urgency we want. Why? Because we're reminding the prospect that their bad writing habits are keeping them from their dream life! That's a powerful motivator. Now, what would motivate *your* prospect to act? Write that down and use it here.

TIME IS OF THE ESSENCE (AGAIN) - EXAMPLE
Eradicate the #1 Bad Habit that's Keeping You from Your Dream Content Writer's Life [CTA:] **YES! I WANT TO MASTER ONLINE WRITING! ENROLL NOW**

11. Why Are We Doing This?

Tell readers why you're passionate about what you're doing/selling. What's your big **why**? Why does it matter?

If you want to, you can include this piece inside your "Details" piece. Of course, maybe you want to really emphasize your/the brand's passion and love for what you provide for your clients. If that's the case, make this a standalone.

In our main sales page example, we included this piece inside the "Details" section. Specifically, I talk about how great content got me to where I am today, and how I want that kind of success for every other writer.

WHY ARE WE DOING THIS? - EXAMPLE

The #1 asset that got me from what I had THEN to what I have NOW?

Great content.

And I mean to continue the trend. In fact, I personally sift through the bulk of writer applicants I get each week (and hire only 1% of them). Out of the bigger group, I cultivate a small team that writes personally for me.

Since 2011, I've worked with my team of writers, first to help them **"unlearn" the bad essay habits** their college professor taught them and then to **learn the art of creating top-notch content.**

Because yes, even the best writers I've worked with carry around a chunk of this bad habit in their systems.

After nine years of intensive training experience, I've come up with: **a polished system that gets writers from**

> **producing clunky, fluff-filled writing to engaging, fun, in-demand content.**
> And I don't mean to keep this system to myself.

12. Paint the Future & Overcome Objections

Help your prospect imagine what their future will be like after they buy. What benefits will follow? What will they get from your offer—both tangibly and intangibly? For example, in a sales page for a course, tangible benefits include things like "zero-fluff video lessons" or "workshop-style tutorials" or "lifetime access." Intangible benefits might include "freedom from the blank page" or "more power in your writing" or "the skills to create content that nets you consistent work and paychecks."

At this point, you can also address their potential objections and why they're wrong. *Be specific.* Why would a prospect object, and how can you soothe those fears? For instance, many writing courses are stuffy and boring. I address this objection by contrasting other courses and how-to books with my course/offer: "Say goodbye to 500-page 'how-to' books stuffed with jargon and tedious, unbroken paragraphs. My zero-frills video lessons take you straight to learning the ABC's of amazing writing in ONE WEEK."

Here's the full example of this section from our real sales page:

What You Get from The Unlearn Essay Writing Course: Your Professional Online Writing Course

This course is your ticket OUT OF the stuffy, clunky essay writing habit and INTO engaging writing your audience craves.

It's chock-full of all the online writing secrets I've discovered in my near-decade of creating content. Secrets which allowed me to grow my content agency Express Writers from a tiny startup worth $0 to a growing brand worth $5 million.

I know the kind of writing clients pay for. You will too, when you finish this course.

You'll get:

Zero-fluff video lessons. Say good-bye to 500-page "how to write" books stuffed with jargon and tedious, unbroken paragraphs. My zero-frills video lessons take you straight to learning the ABC's of amazing writing in ONE WEEK.

Workshop-style tutorials. "Look over my shoulder" and watch me write a piece of content from scratch. In this never-before-seen tutorial style, I take an idea and transform it into a perfectly finessed blog.

My secret sauce for writing, tools, and techniques. With these in your toolbox, you'll never again get stuck staring at a blank Doc and blinking cursor.

A plethora of bonuses and resources. Amp up your writing with power words, writing tools, links to resources and books, and a copywriting formula that'll persuade your audience to do what you want them to.

Lifetime access. Your one-time payment will give you immediate and permanent access to ALL the material in my course. Plus, the evergreen course I'm relaunching later in the year and all the upgrades and updates after that.

Student-only partner discount codes. Get big savings on my favorite tools and products!

A library of templates. Make content creation super easy with 11 content templates to use any time you need them. No more brainstorming your content format – plug your own words into my ready-made templates, and you're good to go!

PAINT THE FUTURE & OVERCOME OBJECTIONS - EXAMPLE

What You Get from The Unlearn Essay Writing Course: Your Professional Online Writing Course

This course is your ticket OUT OF the stuffy, clunky essay writing habit and INTO engaging writing your audience craves.

It's chock-full of all the online writing secrets I've discovered in my near-decade of creating content. Secrets

---

which allowed me to grow my content agency Express Writers from a tiny startup worth $0 to a growing brand worth $5 million.

I know the kind of writing clients pay for. You will too, when you finish this course.

You'll get:

Zero-fluff video lessons. Say good-bye to 500-page "how to write" books stuffed with jargon and tedious, unbroken paragraphs. My zero-frills video lessons take you straight to learning the ABC's of amazing writing in ONE WEEK.

Workshop-style tutorials. "Look over my shoulder" and watch me write a piece of content from scratch. In this never-before-seen tutorial style, I take an idea and transform it into a perfectly finessed blog.

My secret sauce for writing, tools, and techniques. With these in your toolbox, you'll never again get stuck staring at a blank Doc and blinking cursor.

A plethora of bonuses and resources. Amp up your writing with power words, writing tools, links to resources and books, and a copywriting formula that'll persuade your audience to do what you want them to.

Lifetime access. Your one-time payment will give you immediate and permanent access to ALL the material in my course. Plus, the evergreen course I'm relaunching later in the year and all the upgrades and updates after that.

Student-only partner discount codes. Get big savings on my favorite tools and products!

A library of templates. Make content creation super easy with 11 content templates to use any time you need them. No more brainstorming your content format –

plug your own words into my ready-made templates, and you're good to go!

Mega-thorough student workbooks. Make the course your own by writing your answers in these detailed workbooks.

The Unlearn Essay Writing Course Mentorship with Julia: *Included in the course!* Get personal feedback from me on a 1,000-word piece of content you write. I work with you to edit, review, and give the rationale of *why* my suggested edits and revisions will 10x your copy.

13. What to Do Right Now

It's time for the prospect to make a decision. Lay out ALL the details of your program/offer with text and visuals. This is a good place to include pricing.

For our course sales page, we included a full curriculum in this section (which includes a video walk-through) that explains exactly what's inside each course module and what the prospect can expect to learn. After we explain those details, we lay out the pricing for enrollment. Then we add a CTA where they can purchase the course and enroll (more on that in the next section).

The Unlearn Essay Writing Course Curriculum

Course Summary & Inside Look ⌄

Module 1: Unlearn Irrelevant, Weak Writing (with Hands-on Exercises) ⌃

In Module 1 of The Unlearn Essay Writing Course, you'll learn:

- How to dissect a piece of content (the exact checklists I use to label content either good or bad).
- How to turn anything you write into a piece your boss or client will jump over the moon for.
- The step-by-step process for cutting the fluff and gunk from your writing. (You get to watch over my shoulder as I show you how to do it.)
- How to keep up with the ever-changing rules of online grammar (so you always know how to walk the fine line between uneducated and outdated).
- The four steps to ruthless self-editing (turn your icky first draft into a concise, direct, perfectly and professionally polished piece).
- 101 sticky words to never use in your content.

When you press "complete" on Module One you'll:

- Never again write heavy, boring, essay-style content.
- Know what it takes to create content that'll have your boss or client raving for more.
- Have a fully ready, well-polished introduction for your 1,000-word piece.

Module 2: Learn Powerful Online Writing Techniques (with Hands-on Exercises) ⌄

Module 3: Complete Your Article, 8 Bonus Lessons + Featured Guest Joel Klettke, Partner Discounts ⌄

Mentorship Module: Mentor Review, Certification, Bonuses & Partner Discounts ⌄

14. CTA—Let's Talk

Though we're including this as one section, in actuality, you should have multiple CTAs sprinkled throughout your sales page—all of them pointing to ONE place.

For example, on our real-life sales page, we included CTAs at the bottom of almost every major section of text. Some are plain linked text, others are buttons, but they all call the reader to do one thing: "Enroll now."

GET ME IN! ENROLL NOW

Clicking one of these CTAs takes the prospect to our checkout page, where they can buy the course (with a few payment options) and enroll.

Now, for the sales page/offer you're writing, "enroll now" might not be the best CTA. For instance, perhaps a softer sell would work better (e.g., "apply now" where they're taken to an application page to be further qualified as right for your offer, or "let's talk" where they're taken to a page where they can book a call with you/sales).

If you're not sure which CTA will be most effective for your sales page, stick with "let's talk" and go from there. Once you see how that works, you can tweak your CTA accordingly—if customers are readier to buy than you realized, you could switch to "buy now" or "enroll today", for instance.

15. Guarantee & FAQs

Another simple, but necessary, piece of your sales page. This section offers answers to those lingering questions your prospect might have. It also addresses the most-asked questions you get about the offer.

Questions Before Enrolling? FAQ

Can you remind me of the guarantee?

We offer a 14-day money-back guarantee. We want you to take zero percent of the risk — we're taking all of it! But, this course isn't for students who plan to binge-watch all the videos and download all the materials, or simply get their toes wet and "see" without commitment, then decide to ask us for their money back.

To receive our 100% money-back guarantee, there is a requirement: you'll have to study the whole course and complete all the exercises. If you put serious work ethic into it and still don't see improvement in your writing, you're entitled to a full refund.

That being said, I'm super confident this won't happen. When you go through the course, watch the videos, and do the exercises YOU WILL unlearn clunky essay writing and learn the skill to be a top-notch online writer.

Guarantee yourself success with this writing course. Your access unlocks personal mentorship with me. I review and help you edit your piece (as many times as it takes!) until you produce refined, beautiful, client-ready writing.

Take a week to go over this course. Focus on it. Absorb my lessons and do your best with the exercises. Then, spend three weeks testing your new skills. By the end of your guarantee period, you're more likely to email me with your success story than with a refund request.

I'm new to this online writing thing. Is Unlearn Essay Writing going to be too advanced?

Not at all!

Yes, this course teaches the skills leveraged by THE BEST content creators out there. When you finish it, you'll have the full arsenal of writing tools and tricks used by the likes of Jon Morrow and other eight-figure/year earners.

Finally, don't forget to include a guarantee (preferably at the very bottom of the page) to instill confidence in your buyers. For our real sales page, we offer a 14-day money-back guarantee.

The Unlearn Essay Writing Guarantee

We offer a 14-day money-back guarantee. This means we're 1000% committed to your satisfaction!

But remember, this course isn't for students who plan to binge-watch all the videos and download all the materials AND THEN ask me for their money back.

To avail of the money-back guarantee, you'll have to study the whole course and complete all the exercises. If you put serious work ethic into it and still don't see improvement in your writing, you're entitled to a full refund.

16. Bonus: Repel

It may seem counterintuitive, but if your sales page copy does its work, it should not only pull in prospects who are likely to buy—it should also **repel** people who are wrong for the offer/won't buy anyway.

We've already done a bit of this repelling with the "Who It's For/Not For" section (flip back to #6 see examples), but returning to this repellant is a powerful way to end a sales page.

Constructing Your Sales Page

It's time to put all the pieces together. To construct your sales page, I recommend crafting each piece separately, then combining them all on one page and editing as necessary so it all flows together. Feel free to merge sections, rearrange them, and generally build the page as your writer's gut directs you—just don't delete any pieces outright. Refer to the sales page template on the next pages to help you.

Checklist for Sales Page Writing

o   Remember: Long-form sales pages win. When in doubt, go long.

o   BUT—no fluff allowed. Refine, edit, and hone your page as you go. Ensure all the information/copy you've included is essential for your prospect to know.

> o   If you struggle with fluff or unwieldy sentences, study writers known for their succinctness (think Ernest Heminway, Seth Godin, and Brian Dean) and absorb how they put together ideas with no excess words.

> o   Try to eliminate filler words from your copy like:
> - That
> - Just
> - Very
> - Even
> - Really
> - When it comes to
> - So
> - Rather

o   Tinker with the structure of your sales page to your heart's content, but don't remove any elements.

o   Learn the formula for sales page writing and use it with different variations to amp up your offers.

15-Point Sales Page Outline

1. **Hook** – Your attention-grabber. May include the headline, sub-headline, and introductory copy.

2. **Details** – Describe the brand and the offer.

3. **Urgency** – Tell the reader why they should buy now. Let them know why buying now is the best idea (vs. buying later).

4. **Proof** – Provide proof the brand is trustworthy through testimonials from happy customers.

5. **What It Is/What It's Not** – Summarize the offer in crystal clear terms, including what it does NOT include.

6. **Who It's For/Not For** – Reinforce #5 and call out exactly who the offer is for. Then explain who the offer is NOT for.

7. **New Paradigm/Original Concept** – Present the offer in the context of how original it is. If relevant, contrast it with an old way of thinking/doing things that you're subverting with what you're selling.

8. **How You Learned** – How did you (or the brand) gain expertise for what you're selling? Tell that story here.

9. **How It's Working** – How is what you're selling performing exponentially for others? Reinforce #8 by explaining how it's working.

10. **Time Is of the Essence (Again)** – Re-emphasize the urgency of the offer. Why is acting now the BEST idea? What are the benefits your prospect will get from acting now?

11. **Why Are We Doing This**? – Why is the brand passionate about what they sell? What's the big WHY?

12. **Paint the Future & Overcome Objections** – Help your prospect imagine what their future will be like after they buy. What benefits will follow?

13. **What to Do Right Now** – Help the prospect make a decision. Lay out ALL the details of your program/offer with text and visuals.

14. **CTA—Let's Talk** – Include CTAs throughout your sales page linked to ONE place: enroll now, apply now, let's talk, etc.

15. **Guarantee & FAQs** – Include a section for frequently asked questions and the brand's guarantee.

16. **Bonus: Repel** – Reinforce #6 and repel people who will never buy. This is a powerful way to end a sales page.

CHAPTER 6:

Writing for YouTube

Wait a minute. Why, in a book about content writing, do we have an entire chapter devoted to *YouTube*?

Because creating video content isn't just about the videos, themselves. The content that *surrounds* those videos is equally as important.

Search engines and other content-serving platforms aren't sophisticated enough to understand raw video footage—yet. If you simply post a video with no written content attached to it, those platforms will have no way to index it. They won't know what it's about or what keywords to associate it with, and thus they won't serve it to users searching for that topic. And that's the whole point, my friends.

That means video content NEEDS written content to go with it, whether you post to platforms like YouTube, Vimeo, Wistia, etc., or embed videos on your website.

Search engines and video platforms look for contextual clues to figure out what your video is about.

Provide those clues in the written content that surrounds your video, and you'll have a better chance of your audience finding it. If you think of your video content as buried treasure, that means the written content attached to it (the video title and description, for example) are like the map that helps people discover it.

And, it goes without saying, but your videos themselves also need to be good: relevant to your chosen topic, high-quality, and targeted to the right audience. All the optimization in the world won't save a terrible, irrelevant, useless video. (Spoiler: Content writing can help you there, too.)

Because video content matters immensely. 87% of marketers say video has helped them increase their website traffic. 82% say video helped them improve dwell time (the length of time a visitor spends looking at a web page), and 86% say it helped them generate leads.[33] And don't forget, consumers love video. They are twice as likely to share video content vs. any other type of content. And a staggering 92% of all internet users watch videos weekly.[34]

What about YouTube? It is the second-most-used search engine after Google. It's also the largest and most popular video platform in the world, with over 2

---

[33] Wyzowl. (2022). "The State of Video Marketing 2022." https://wyzowl.s3.eu-west-2.amazonaws.com/pdfs/Wyzowl-Video-Survey-2022.pdf

[34] Statista. (2022, Dec. 9). "Most popular video content type worldwide in 2nd quarter 2022, by weekly usage reach." https://www.statista.com/statistics/1254810/top-video-content-type-by-global-reach/

billion monthly active users.[35] For those reasons, in this brief chapter, we'll focus exclusively on writing for YouTube, including how to write video outlines and how to optimize your videos with written content (like titles and descriptions). We'll even show you how to use ChatGPT to speed up video creation!

How to Optimize YouTube Videos with Written Content

Now that you know how important written content is for your videos, how do you incorporate it strategically for SEO so your audience can find the content and understand its relevancy for their needs? Let's explore, piece by piece.

Title

First up, your video title. Every single video on YouTube has a title. Just like with SEO blogs, your title helps viewers understand what your video is about *and* can help convince them to watch it. And, if your title contains a focus keyword, YouTube can more easily rank your video for that keyword.

That's why, before I create any video content for YouTube, I always start by researching a good keyword and matching topic that will appeal to my target audience.

---

[35] YouTube Official Blog. (n.d.) "YouTube for Press." https://blog.youtube/press/

Need some pointers on YouTube SEO and keyword research? Want to know my YouTube process from start to finish? Check out my exhaustive guide: **contenthacker.com/youtube**

For example, for one of my videos, my keyword was "how to write press releases." Thus, my title was "How to Write Press Releases (with Examples)." (Bonus: Title your video file with the keyword, too!)

As you come up with keyword-optimized titles for your videos, remember to keep them simple and clear. However, you should also use some of the headline-writing skills you picked up in earlier chapters of this handbook!

Particularly, try to make your headline engaging to spark curiosity and interest in your potential viewers. Think in terms of hooking them, but also be descriptive and tell them what to expect without overpromising or falling into clickbait territory. Those things ultimately will make your audience more likely to watch your video.

Description

Next, create a keyword-optimized YouTube video description. This piece of written content shows up in the gray box directly underneath your video title and channel name.

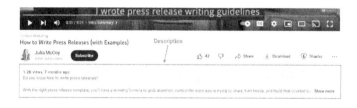

The description is KEY for optimizing your video, so don't phone in this part. Here is a basic outline to follow, including how to write each piece. (Want to see each example in action? Check out my YouTube video here: **https://youtu.be/L8haWVtOjPk**)

1. **Hook** – Describe what your video is about. Include any keywords here, especially your focus keyword near the beginning. Write 1-3 paragraphs, max. Remember to get specific and tell your potential viewer what benefits they'll receive from watching your video (what will they learn? How will it help them in their work/life?). Example:

1,214 views Premiered May 16, 2022
Do you know how to write press releases?

With the right press release template, you'll have a winning formula to grab attention, control the story you're trying to share, turn heads, and build that coveted buzz.

Watch and learn:

• The definition of a press release and why you should write them
• The ROI of providing press release writing as a service
• How to write a press release, with a press release template to help you with formatting
• The 5 basic questions every news release should answer
• Press release examples and types

Read the blog with more examples: https://contenthacker.com/press-relea...

2. **Chapters** – Write out at least three timestamps for the most important sections of your video. Use the 00:00 format, and clearly label what each video "chapter" is about. (Note: YouTube also has a feature for adding automatic chapters which you can then edit. Choose the method that works best for you.) Adding chapters is fantastic for usability, and Google can even pull these when they show your video in search results. Example:

3. **Footer** – Each video description should include a pre-written snippet of text that promotes the creator. This can be copied across video descriptions. Include a short bio, what they do, how they've done it, who they serve, and any major career highlights that back up their expertise (e.g., books they've written, podcasts they host, etc.). Example:

Who's Julia McCoy?

I'm a serial entrepreneur, 5x bestselling author, and now, business strategy coach.

I've made money on the internet since I was 13. At 19 years old, I started a writing agency with my last $75. by the age of 30, I exited that exact business for 7 figures. We grew to 5,000 clients reached, a marketplace leader, and over 100 people on staff.

I hate sleaze and slime used to "sell" on the internet. My businesses are living, breathing, ten-year proof that there are better ways.

At my brand The Content Hacker, I help creative entrepreneurs get their strategy, skills & systems down for massive revenue.

My elite coaching program, The Content Transformation© System, will teach you exactly how to build & scale a market-proof, self-sustaining business you love, with a content based game plan that will help you last for years to come.

We're here to help you grow, the right way.

Want to learn more? → Watch my free class: https://contenthacker.com/training/
Book a free strategy session → https://contenthacker.com/book-call/

Subscribe to new content: https://contenthacker.com/subscribe/
Read my books: https://www.amazon.com/Julia-McCoy/e/...
Connect on Instagram: https://instagram.com/thejuliamccoy/

4. **Hashtags** – End your description with 3-5 relevant hashtags that connect to your topic and focus keyword. E.g., #pressreleasewriting, #contentwriting, #contentmarketing, etc.

And, just to give you a full example of what this looks like, here's another description pulled from a different YouTube video on my channel:

YOUTUBE DESCRIPTION EXAMPLE

Thinking of starting your own content business this year? Need to make money online and create a business that you love running?

In the last ten years, I've assembled my own business and team of 100+ people at Express Writers. It's not easy, and it's not for everyone, but it is incredibly rewarding.

Here are some of my best tips on how to start your very own content business. There has never been a better time to get into content than NOW!

CHAPTERS

01:10 Use my 4 L's to build a business you love: Love, Learn, Labor, Level Up

01:55 Why you should start a content business: Content marketing is set to be worth

BILLIONS

02:22 Find out what you LOVE to do in writing

02:49 LEARN all you can about what you're about to do, from real practitioners

05:13 WHO to learn from

06:43 LABOR: do the work

07:35 Level Up: hit your next level and grow

08:17 My 3 P's to be successful long-term

→ SUBSCRIBE: https://www.youtube.com/juliamccoy

→ COACHING FOR CREATIVE ENTREPRENEURS:

https://contenthacker.com/transformation

I'm a serial entrepreneur, 5x bestselling author, and now, I teach creative entrepreneurs the

skills and strategy of starting and scaling a successful digital business from scratch. (Learn

more: → https://contenthacker.com/transformation)

I've made money on the internet since I was 13. At 19 years old, I started a writing agency

with $75; by the age of 30, I exited for 7 figures. We grew to 5,000 clients reached; a

marketplace leader; and over 100 people on staff.

I hate sleaze and slime used to "sell" on the internet. My businesses are living, breathing, ten-year proof that there are better ways.

At my brand The Content Hacker, I help creative entrepreneurs get their strategy, skills & systems down for massive revenue. I help you reprogram yourself to leave all the worker mentality behind and grow into CEO, and then I teach you the strategic steps to run a multi-6, 7-figure digital company.

My elite coaching program, The Content Transformation© System, will teach you exactly how to build & scale a market-proof, self-sustaining business you love, with a content-based game plan that will help you last for years to come.

Want to learn more? →
https://contenthacker.com/transformation/

_____

Subscribe to new content:
https://contenthacker.com/subscribe/
Read my books: https://www.amazon.com/Julia-McCoy/e/B01EGB9EDW
Connect on Instagram:
https://instagram.com/fementrepreneur

#JuliaMcCoy #ContentHacking
#ContentMarketing #SEO

Bonus: Blog Post

Want to take optimization further? Consider creating a matching blog post on your website to maximize video + website content together.

When you plan out your video content and search for keywords/topics, just extend that search a bit for blog SEO. For example, search a YouTube SEO tool for a good video keyword, then look up that same keyword in a standard SEO tool like Mangools KWFinder or Semrush. Find a match (or a near-match) and create a blog post on the same topic as your video. Then embed your video in the post on your site!

Want to see an example of a symbiotic YouTube video + blog post working in harmony? Check out my blog/video combo on how to create long-form content: **contenthacker.com/how-to-create-long-form-content**

How to Create a Video Outline

Ah, here we are again. Back to outlining.

If you dread creating outlines, it's time to get comfortable with it, fast—because even the simplest outline can help you immensely for ANY kind of content creation… even for videos on YouTube.

Think of your outline as your strategy for shaping your content, no matter the format. Your outline can give a defined shape and structure to videos as well as the more obvious blogs, long-form content, and even shorter formats like emails and social posts.

When we talk about creating an outline for a video, don't get caught up in making it complex, such as timing what you'll say to the second. You don't even have to write a word-for-word script of what you'll say and when (unless you *want* to—if that makes you feel more confident, be my guest). Instead, I recommend keeping it loose and simple.

For my videos, I create a very rough 3-5 point outline that lists out the most important talking points I want to remember to cover.

How do I find these talking points? Here's a quick rundown of my process:

1. In advance, research a good video keyword/topic, related to your audience's pain points or interests, using a YouTube SEO tool like VidIQ.[36]

2. Watch one or two videos on that topic on YouTube for inspiration (what comes up during a search).

3. Get ideas of talking points that are unique/different from what's already on YouTube. Maximize expertise and your differentiation factor and learn into inspiration for a unique perspective.

After that, create your simple, 3-5 point video outline from what you learned from the above research. Here's an example from a video I created:

---

[36] https://vidiq.com

YOUTUBE VIDEO OUTLINE EXAMPLE

KEYWORD/TOPIC: how to start your content business

TITLE: How to Start Your Content Business: Make Money Online

TAKEAWAYS:

1. Love: find out what you love doing in the writing industry
2. Learn: learn all you can about what you love doing
3. Labor: get to work knocking on doors (pitching!) and getting money to get going; build better and better skills
4. Level Up: scale, hire, and grow as your income and clients grow)

How to Use ChatGPT for Faster Video Creation, by Owen Hemsath

This genius mini-guide comes from video marketer **Owen Hemsath** *of Acceleratus Media. Here's his method to use ChatGPT to create faster, better video content for YouTube.*

Imagine a person who has read every single book, every article, every video, in every language, and can recite it all back to you in minutes—that's ChatGPT.

Some people don't get the vision.

They see it as a shiny object or a simple distraction to the existing order.

We disagree.

WHEN USED CORRECTLY—AI will allow you to reach more people with more thoughtful content and enhance the human experience.

Have you ever wanted to share a message but couldn't find the words?

Have you ever wanted to make a video but didn't have time to research it?

AI solves that problem.

But...

You need to know how to use it.

ChatGPT is based on prompts and what you ask it to do. If you ask bad questions, you'll get bad robotic or inaccurate answers.

Sometimes you may need to ask two or three prompts in the right order to get what you need.

Writing prompts are key.

My team has made a cheat sheet with the best prompts to type in for video content creation.

How to use these prompts to create content without watering yourself down:

- **Tip #1**: Use it for the initial drafting that you revise:
    - o Use the outputs as bones for your content. The outputs will help your own ideas. Your expertise comes in to bring in the personality and the valuable meat.
- **Tip #2**: Use it to revise your original content.
    - o Give it your current content and use the technology to take where you are weak and use AI to help you make you strong.

The more specifics you can give it, the better it works.

- **Tip #3**: Give it scripts/copy.
  - o You can give it scripts of your current content on YouTube at *youtubetranscript.com*

Video Content Creation and Optimization Prompts for ChatGPT

- Can you rewrite this title into 5 intriguing YouTube video titles?: [type your current title here]
- Can you write a fun introduction to my video on the topic of [paste topic here]?
- Please summarize: [copy and paste your lengthy text].
- Please make this sound more intriguing: [type boring text for hooks, intros, etc.].
- Can you reword the text to make it sound like an [X person from XYZ? Please include the word [keyword here]: [type your text here].
- Can you write a YouTube description box copy for this video: [type title here or script].
  - o Can you rewrite it to make it sound [smarter/funnier/sassier/sexier/etc.]?
- I want to create a video series on the topic of [X for Audience]. What are 10 video topics I could include in this series?
- Write me a YouTube script on [type topic and angle here].

- o Can you summarize this into a video outline instead?
- o Can you expand on or go into more detail about [xyz topic]?

- Write me an outline for a YouTube video on the topic of [type topic and angle here].
- Can you give me a few three-word thumbnail text ideas for the YouTube video titled, "[paste your video title here]"?

Here's an example of how to use the prompts.

- Open ChatGPT (chat.openai.com) and log in.
- In the text box, write your prompt and fill in the brackets [ ] with your information.

- Hit "enter" and watch ChatGPT write.

- If you're not happy with the output, hit "Regenerate response" to let ChatGPT try again. Or, rephrase your initial prompt. You can also ask ChatGPT to edit the output in a specific style.

Can you edit this introduction to be more serious?

 Of course! Here's a revised version:

"Good day, and welcome to our informative video on the subject of SEO blog writing. If you're looking to improve your website's search engine rankings and increase your online visibility, you've come to the right place. In this video, we'll be discussing key concepts and best practices for effective SEO blog writing. Our goal is to provide you with a comprehensive understanding of the subject, so that you can make informed decisions and achieve your desired results. Please grab a notebook and get ready to take some notes as we delve into the world of SEO blog writing."

For more cutting-edge thoughts and advice on video marketing that generates income and impacts your following, subscribe to Owen on YouTube at **@OwenVideo1**, or read his blog at *thevideomarketingschool.com*.

Checklist for Writing for YouTube

o Create written content for YouTube to help both viewers and the YouTube algorithm find your videos.

o Research keywords and topics for YouTube videos using the right tools.

o Look at what videos already exist for your keyword/topic on YouTube. From these, draw inspiration on what you could do/say differently that speaks to your target audience. Lean on your expertise and differentiation factor to come up with a unique perspective on the topic.

o Create a compelling video title that uses your focus keyword. Keep it clear and simple.

o Write a description for each video that you post. Include key elements like a hook, chapters, and a footer.

o Outline what you'll say in each video you create. Your outline doesn't have to be complex or fancy— a simple 3-5-point list of talking points will do.

Writing for YouTube Outlines

Outline for Shaping Your Video Content

Title: Clear, simple title that contains your keyword.

Takeaways: 3-5 talking points, or the most important points you'll make about the topic.

YouTube Description Outline

Hook:

- 1-3 paragraphs, maximum
- Describe what the video is about, clearly. Use any keywords, if there are keywords your video is about.

Chapters:

- In the 00:00 format, write out timestamps for important parts of your video. This is fantastic for usability and will show up in Google search results for the focus keyword your video is about.

Footer:

- Include a pre-loaded footer that promotes the creator that you can copy/paste here. Include books, bio, and a short summary of what it is they do, as well as who they do it for (target audience).

Hashtags:

- End with 3-5 hashtags that are on the topic. Example: #SEO

VIDEO CREATION PROMPTS FOR CHATGPT

- Can you rewrite this title into 5 intriguing YouTube video titles?: [type your current title here]
- Can you write a fun introduction to my video on the topic of [paste topic here]?
- Please summarize: [copy and paste your lengthy text].
- Please make this sound more intriguing: [type boring text for hooks, intros, etc.].
- Can you reword the text to make it sound like an [X person from XYZ]? Please include the word [keyword here]: [type your text here].
- Can you write a YouTube description box copy for this video: [type title here or script].
  - o Can you rewrite it to make it sound [smarter/funnier/sassier/sexier/etc.]?
- I want to create a video series on the topic of [X for Audience]. What are 10 video topics I could include in this series?
- Write me a YouTube script on [type topic and angle here].

- o Can you summarize this into a video outline instead?
- o Can you expand on or go into more detail about [xyz topic]?
- Write me an outline for a YouTube video on the topic of [type topic and angle here].
- Can you give me a few three-word thumbnail text ideas for the YouTube video titled, "[paste your video title here]"?

CONCLUSION

We can't wrap up a book about content writing without talking about the storm on all of our horizons: AI.

Writers, it's a brand new world out there for us. A *brave* new world. How will you move forward from here?

If you truly want to stay relevant and valuable in the face of AI writing software, you need to **build your skills** beyond what an AI can do.

Any artificial intelligence tool can write at a general level. If you stay at that level, your job will be gone.

So—become the master.

Know your stuff well enough to write in the position of "thought leader."

Understand what profitable content looks like. Understand how to create it for a multitude of brands and clients, for a diverse array of target audiences.

Know in your gut what your magic human touch can do when you apply it to ANY type of content, AI-created or not.

Don't sit back on your laurels and let AI do the work. **Be the expert who drives the AI.** Be the mastermind pulling the strings. Without your guidance, AI can only produce decent content. WITH your guidance, AI can produce **pure gold**.

Go from human-only production to **AIO** (optimizing AI output), and you'll be *faster, better, and more efficient* than any other type of writer on the planet. We're in new times.

I hope this book gave you a solid baseline, a roadmap to content creation you can follow over and over to reach that pinnacle.

Brand owners, you're a part of this brave new world, too.

The fact that you're holding this book, or that you put it in the hands of your AIO (artificial intelligence optimization) writer, speaks volumes about you and your approach to content marketing.

You still believe in the power of human creativity, ingenuity, and passion. And that is what will set you apart from the other businesses that will pump out AI content without discretion or the human touch.

You know your audience deserves the best content you can give them. It's also how you will become known, earn search engine rankings, bring more visitors and leads to your website, and ultimately drive more sales.

The best content is human-powered, AI-assisted. I hope this book served as your guide to powering up your human writers.

Go forth, and be awesome.

ABOUT THE AUTHOR

Julia McCoy is an 8x author and a leading strategist around creating exceptional content and presence that lasts online. As the VP of Marketing at Content at Scale, she leads marketing for one of the fastest-growing AI content writing tools for SEO marketers on the planet. She's been named in the top 30 of all content marketers worldwide, is the founder of Content Hacker, and exited a 100-person writing agency she spent 10 years building with a desire to help marketers, teams, and entrepreneurs find the keys of online success and revenue growth without breaking.

Read her eight books on Amazon, including a non-fiction memoir of her life growing up in and escaping a radical cult: Woman Rising, A True Story.

Connect with Julia on Twitter and Instagram: @JuliaEMcCoy.

Visit Julia's site: ContentHacker.com

Learn about Content at Scale: ContentHacker.com/AI or ContentatScale.ai

Email the author: julia@contenthacker.com

Made in the USA
Monee, IL
17 June 2023

35737324R00144